MISSED THE BOAT

Allan Birkin has done many a job. In his 62 years so far, he's been a caddy, pot collector, car cleaner, butcher, joiner, builder, drummer, singer-songwriter and blue stand-up comedian.

He also had a little dabble at being a TV presenter, took roles in various reality TV programmes, and has been an extra in everything from *Crossroads* to *Brookside*.

This all culminates in the position he finds himself today – attempting to be an author.

After starting out on a screenplay, *Why Are We Here?* (the next big thing), he's almost at the completion stage of four or five fiction and non-fiction books.

These will be published under the Words Are Life umbrella making all Allan Birkin's work readily available for the masses to read.

Missed the Boat tells Allan's story. It's a journey that starts out when he's a drummer and progresses to him being a singer-songwriting front man and onto being a slightly popular blue stand-up comedian (following in the footsteps of Bernard Manning and Chubby Brown).

Life on the road wasn't easy and is certainly not for everyone. All those years on the road in pubs, clubs discotheques, hotels and holiday camps… and travelling 1000s of miles have left him even today nursing one hell of a massive hangover.

While at the top of his game, Allan Birkin quickly realised his act would never amount to more than just a good night's entertainment, so took the decision to call it a day.

He was honest in saying if he spent another 50 years doing exactly the same thing, he would still only be exactly where he was that day.

MISSED THE BOAT

You don't have to be funny, to be funny

Allan Birkin

"If at first you don't succeed, that's the end of Parachuting"

It is often said that two heads are better than one. Well, believe me, they are not wrong! I'm talking about a guy who has been one of my sidekicks for ever and a day. He's multi-talented and could sell sand to an Arab and ice to an Eskimo. He's a singer, a very funny guy, and very knowledgeable on everything from birth to death and from planet earth to the very edges of the universe… To top that, he's a whizz on the computer. When I showed him my cover to this book, he couldn't help himself and had to create his own version, so I thought it only best that I include it inside this book.

All the best to you, my good friend, Mr Anthony Martin.

ALLAN BIRKIN

At the present moment, the author has no
further titles available for purchase,
but please email adb180960@hotmail.com
with any enquiries regarding this
book or future titles.

"I apologise in advance if some of the swear words used in this book cause offence. It wasn't my intention to cause offence, but the words were needed to express my thoughts correctly."

ALLAN BIRKIN

MISSED THE BOAT

www.wordsarelife.co.uk

A13 OMS PRESS

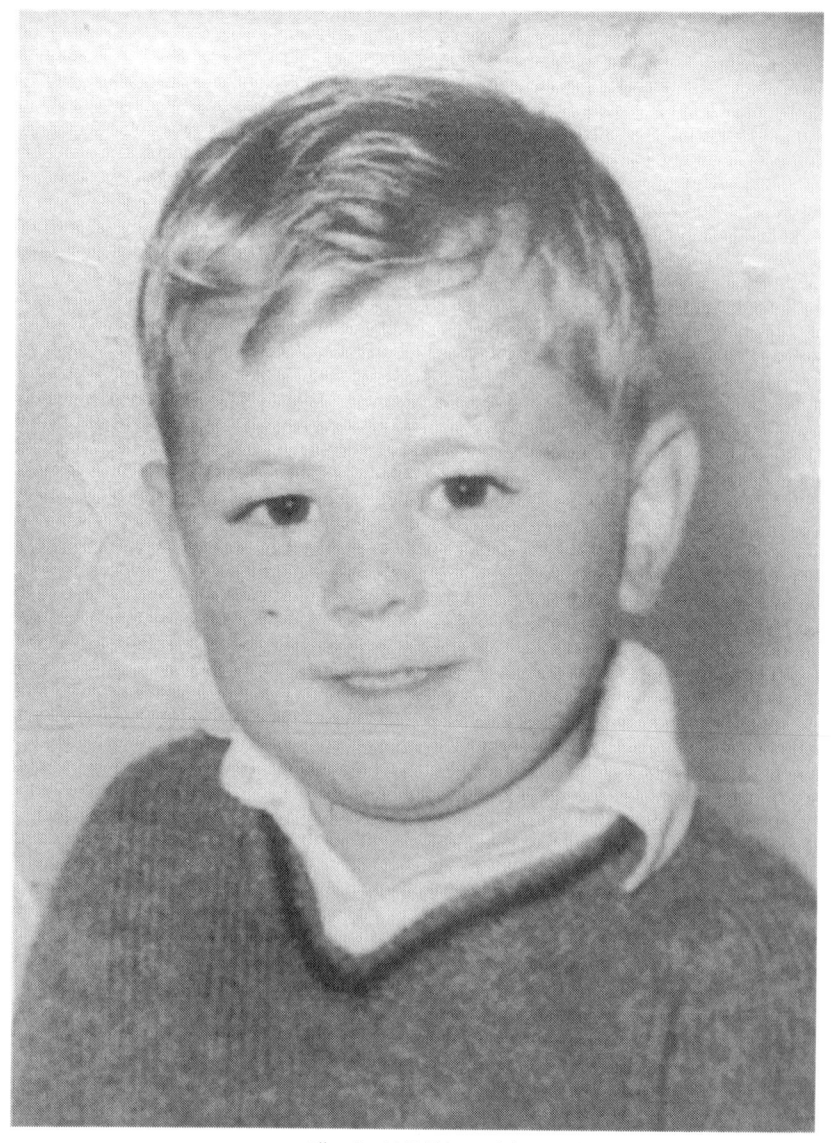

Allan David Birkin, aged three.

MISSED THE BOAT
ALLAN BIRKIN

WORDS ARE LIFE PUBLISHING

First published in Great Britain in 2022 by
Words Are Life
10 Chester Place,
Adlington, Chorley,
PR6 9RP

lesley@wordsarelife.co.uk

Electronic and paperback versions available for purchase on Amazon.

Copyright (c) Allan Birkin and Words Are Life.

A13 OMS PRESS

All rights reserved. Without limiting the rights under copyright reserved above, no part of this publication may be reproduced, stored or introduced into a retrieval system, or transmitted, in any form or by any means (electronic, mechanical, photocopying, recording or otherwise), without the prior written permission of both the copyright owner and the publisher of this book.

Cover photograph: Sydney, 2013, Allan Birkin.

Back page cover: Allan, Shani, Ashley and Allan Jnr.

The Amateur Furrytographer since 1971.

WHO THE BOOK'S FOR

This book was written by me and is a present for all those interested in reading its contents.

I hope you enjoy it, even more so if you bought it, and especially if I've made a few quid although that's definitely not my intention (honestly).

(I will however add that although I went to Salford grammar school, that's as far as my English went. I didn't get any GCEs, so I make my apologies that my phrasing or punctuation is not very good. I will just say I tried my best, and get the pre-emptive strike in before all the educated busybodies point it out.)

They say that you can choose your friends but not your family. As hard as I've tried over the years, I've come to realise that it's impossible to please everybody. So, just like the audiences I've worked in front of for many a year, it's better to work to the majority and not the minority.

To complete this book, I've turned to the Words Are Life publishing umbrella with their expertise.

It's where I find myself today.

Thank you!

Allan Birkin

ALLAN BIRKIN

CONTENTS

1. Foreword
2. How it all Started
3. Opportunity Knocked
4. Heckler or Dickhead
5. Comedy Heroes
6. The Next Great Gag
7. Lucky Lad
8. Working With Strippers
9. Remembering all the Jokes
10. Can I Just Tell You This One?
11. Places to Work
12. Taking a Break
13. My Advice (Jack of all Trades)
14. TV Work
15. The Roadies
16. Sportsmen's Dinners
17. Material
18. Harry Barnes
19. Just Do Us Half an Hour
20. One Last Shot

ALLAN BIRKIN

MISSED THE BOAT

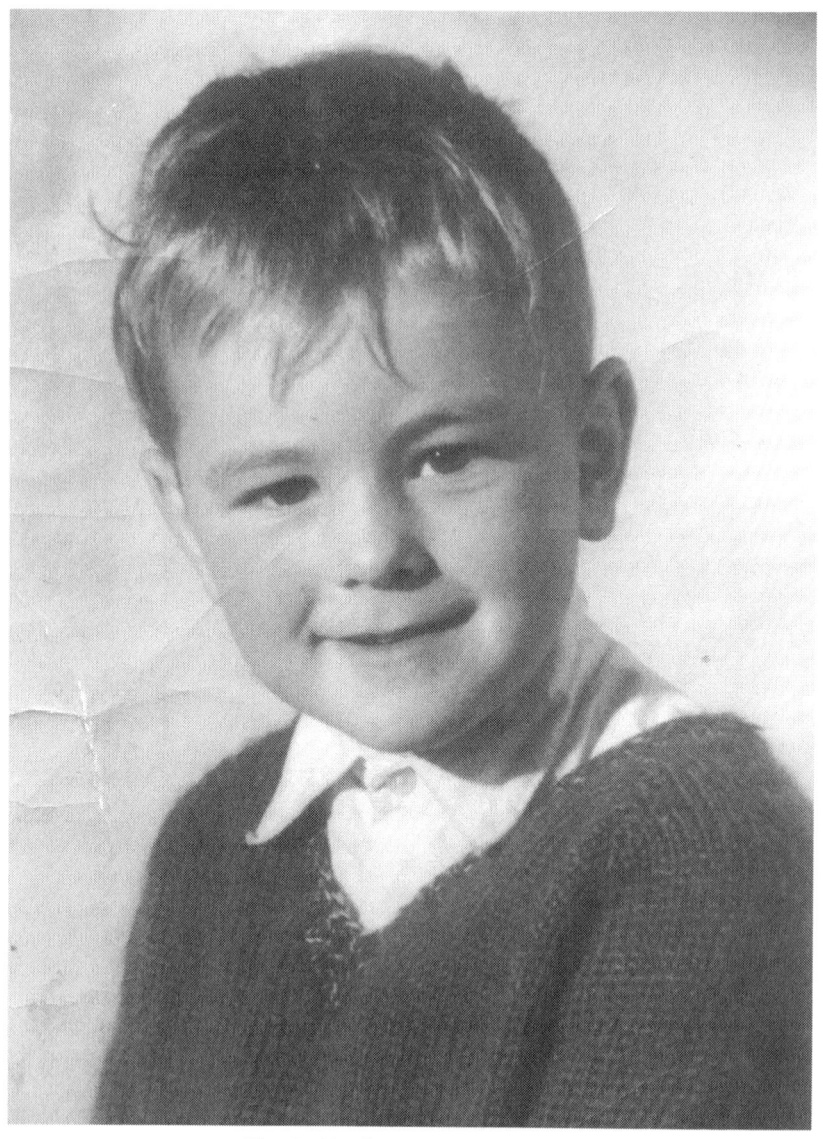

Allan David Birkin, getting cuter by the year.

TAKE NOTE

IF I COULD WALK OUT THE FRONT DOOR STRAIGHT ONto a stage, pick up the microphone and entertain, come off stage and walk straight back through the front door, there would be no problem. Without a doubt, I would stay working the stage till the day I pop my clogs.

But it isn't like that.

You pack your car, drive to the gig, spend ages finding it (no sat nav in them days – how did we survive?), drag your gear in, set it all up, do a sound check, wait around while the bingo takes place, endure the raffles, get changed then perform, change again, drop your gear, reload the car back up drive home, get KFC on the way, fill up with petrol, arrive home, unload your car then have a goodnight brew.

I would spend all day and every day prior to a gig worrying and thinking about a valid excuse as to why and how I could get out of actually doing it. I'd be thinking up excuses I could use to cover my tracks as to why I didn't want to do it!

It was time to call it a day.

1
FOREWORD

IF I FAIL TO LEARN ANYTHING ELSE IN THE TIME I have left of my life, one thing I have learnt, and do feel I know for sure is – I missed the boat.

In this day and age, or as we term it, the 21st century, television gives us the likes of *The X Factor*, *The Voice*, and *Britain's Got Talent*, which are all programmes designed to find new talent, or as launch pads for existing artistes. If I'm honest with myself, though... not only do I have no voice, I only have a face for radio, so that rules me out.

I am the ultimate live performer. My act and the way I perform just wouldn't have come across the same on television. Missed the boat… Yes, missed the boat is an expressive term I would use for not making it to the pinnacle of the showbiz world.

After years of trying and exploring almost every avenue open to me, the conclusion was made to "Give it up as a bad job, laddie boy".

As 2012 draws to a close, I have just arrived home from a gig. I pause for a moment, then realise that gig was a confirmation of what I first realised in 2002 and then had confirmed to me fully in 2007. Confirmation that life was almost definitely a young man's game. I'm no defeatist, but it really is.

In 2002, I read an article (in the *Manchester Evening News)* saying that auditions were taking place on Oxford Road in the city centre of my home town of Manchester, for *STOMP*.

STOMP is the very popular drumming, dancing and theatre show. All dressed in big boots and baggy clothes, and with those big boots and baggy clothes you find a way, using your hands and feet, to bang on everything from the backyard dustbin, to the pots and pans that hide inside our kitchen cupboards.

The *STOMP* theatre show has the luxury of playing to packed out audiences all over the world, albeit in the various genres of both male and female ensembles.

The term "Life is a young man's game" is a little gem I finally realised was true as I auditioned for this very show. When I saw the advert, I thought "Piece of piss, this. I can drum, I have rhythm, and if need be, I can dance a little, and most importantly I'm still pretty active, even at the ripe old age of 42. What I didn't realise though, was that my brain was a lot slower and wouldn't fit the audition's criteria of learning on the spot.

Learning new things instantly was a definite no-no for me. The youngsters may well have been able to pick it all up immediately, but I, on the other hand needed a few hours to go over it and over it – a luxury the STOMPers were in no way prepared to offer. They hadn't the time and possibly also didn't have the inclination. I was ushered from the audition room with the echoes of "Don't call us, we'll call you…". I wondered for a split second then asked if they had my number. "No," was the reply, "But don't worry. If we need you, we will guess it".

Ha ha, "Smart arse motherfuckers". That's a line I took from Ross from *Friends*. Like I've said before, there's nothing new in comedy.

A young me. Certainly no model. This was from my TV work portfolio.

In 2007, I did what was by then to me just a routine Gents Night consisting of a comedian and two female strippers. They were not strippers, by the way, but actresses (in their eyes only, of course). I've done so many of these shows, I could both run them and do them in my sleep. Basically, you start the show at 9pm and run it till 9.50, then you have about a 25-minute break for pie n peas and whatever raffles are going on etc. Then you do the second half starting about 10.15, which goes on till 11:05. During these two sessions, the females are meant to appear twice, once in each half. Then the comic links it all together, giving the punters value for their dollar!

Well that's how it's supposed to go, but then along came the bullshit-spouting younger strippers with their tits sticking out, telling the organisers with their puppy dog eyes and seduction techniques (because all us men are suckers for a sexy chick with big tits) that they will only do one long spot each. It totally fucks up the format of the show. Their one long spot is seven minutes ish. Long, my arse! One spot should be almost ten minutes, and a long spot should be 15 to 20. Without this, it leaves the comic trying to stretch the show. Doing stand up for 40 minutes is no mean feat, and doing it for almost 70-80 is very difficult. So, I arrived at the gig in Ashton-under-Lyne where I soon discovered the girls had already suckered the organiser with their 'one long spot' bullshit. Well, that time I wasn't prepared to play ball, especially when these actresses had already been acting for all of ten minutes. So I found the organiser and thus begin to have a stern word in his shell-like.

"I'm sorry, mate, but if you're prepared to accept the girls only performing the one spot each, I can only do 45/50 minutes around their spots, which means your show is over at ten past ten. When you're working as a comic, to do two longer sets is difficult. You have to build on it and keep your audience's attention. To do it four times is near impossible, and (truth be known) why should I even to attempt to work that hard when the girls so obviously couldn't give a shit?"

I felt guilty saying that, but I'd had enough of cheeky-bastard strippers not performing what they were getting paid to do!

When the organiser left the room, I said to the girls "You know you're booked for two spots each, not just the one. You're completely fucking the show up. I don't mean to preach, but I've been doing this show a very long time, ladies. Come on, play ball."

"We do one long spot," said one girl, while the other muttered, "If you've been doing this job a long time, you haven't learnt much have you?"

Cheeky pair of bitches. I was fuming. I left that place at 10.15 and vowed I was done working with female strippers. Needless to say, I've rarely worked more than a handful of those shows ever since. And that is definitely my choice.

So, it was 2012 and I was home. The kettle was on, the telly was up and running, a sandwich made, and I was all relaxed, eating, drinking and watching whatever was on. I began to ponder, especially after that night's show. I was a Ladies Night, the complete opposite to the Gents Night. Women are mental and they love a good time, like to dance and get leathered (drunk). Yes, I've done lots of these and I love them.

I don't mind on these shows if the male strippers do one spot each because, unlike the ladies, the guys' one long spot is often 15/20 minutes. They really do give the punters value for money.

When you work with professionals it makes your job a lot easier. I didn't have to fill the night with jokes and I could spend half the night singing, because (as we all know) women love a good sing song.

Over the years, I've done some great Ladies Nights, after all, I'm a hot-blooded male and what man in his right mind wouldn't want to be surrounded by a crowd of horny, inebriated, sexy girls with their mothers and grannies, all hell bent on having a good time… Yes, yes, yes, I loved it.

Unfortunately, that Ladies Night wasn't one of the good ones. The audience was an extension of a college A-level class, each person being about 17, 18 or 19-years-old. Not only did they not understand most of the jokes I told, but the songs I had in my locker to perform were dead and buried long before most of the crowd were even born. Most Ladies Nights end with 45 minutes of disco pumping the dance floor till the girls are all sweaty and sticky. Us men were normally there to witness, but I wasn't on that occasion. I was sat in my lounge at home with a sandwich and coffee as the DJ played the final song.

I was at a crossroads. For years, I trod the boards in search of what we artistes call 'fame and fortune'. Not only was I tired of trying to achieve it, I was also tired of realising it just wasn't going to happen.

As they say, I'd been there and done it, and even if I spent the next 30 years on the road, the fame and fortune weren't going to happen. Not even if it meant driving down that road for 30 years in my favourite ever car: my S-reg, two-year-old, orange with a black vinyl roof, Ford Capri.

My Ford Capri. My favourite-ever car.

There was absolutely no disillusionment. Not one drop. It isn't, or wasn't, that I wasn't good enough, because I know or knew that I could hold my own. It was just that, for me, it hadn't worked. So, just like a lot of other great acts who didn't quite make it… I MISSED THE BOAT.

I have no regrets, though. Absolutely, none at all. I really can't complain. Doing stand-up was far better than hanging doors and building roofs all day. Half of me wanted to chuck in the towel, while the other half wanted me to get back on the horse so to speak, giving it maybe one last shot.

As I was drinking and eating, my phone bleeped and a text came through with a joke. It was funny and I thought for a moment that I couldn't wait to be on stage to tell it.

This book will give you a little insight into how things started, where I went and, hopefully by the time I get to the end of the book, where I am going next…

Enjoy xxx

2
HOW IT ALL STARTED

IF YOU ASK ME HOW IT ALL STARTED, THE ANSWER'S simple. As soon as one lesson finished at good old Salford Grammar School, I would hurryingly race to the next lesson. Hopefully, it would give me a spare two or three minutes in which I would have time to re-arrange the tilted school desks all around me. Then I would bang like fuck, thinking I was the next Cozy Powell, Eric Delaney or Buddy Rich, and in plain English… The World's Greatest Drummer.

Occasionally, I would get to class and the teacher would already be there, and I'd be thinking "Bastard"!

The school desks.

Banging Birkin.

Back in those days, if it had a sound to be discovered by banging on it, I would bang, bang, bang. "Shut the fuck up, Birkin" was all I ever heard from all and sundry in all directions, and that included the people in my own house. Haha.

Yes, All drummers are mental.

On many occasions, I used to carry my whole drum kit to the playing fields at the back of the houses where I lived, in Lower Kersal. I'd set my kit up so I could make as much noise as possible without disturbing a soul. That was a buzz.

I would tap on anything and everything, and still do it to this day wherever I am. If I'm in the kitchen, I tap on the worktop in front of the sink, and have my right foot tapping on the floor.

Of all the things I ever tapped on, my favourite was the metal shelf in the old K6 red telephone box. The sound that came from the shelf was amazing. Yes, I'm a geek! But I so loved the sound it made.

The old K6 telephone box. The parcel shelf had the best sound ever.

My first real drum kit was a right old pile of pots and pans, probably worth about £10 all in. I've no idea where I even got them from. All I know is that it felt like I was a *Steptoe and Son* drummer, but I didn't care. I just wanted to play, no matter what.

To this very day, even though I've been off on different tangents and very rarely have a good old knock on the drums, it still remains an ambition of mine to play on a miked-up drum kit in a big theatre. A miked-up drum kit is a sound in itself, so I've not given up on that one just yet!

I remember as a kid taking over my dad's pride and joy shed, and covering the inside walls in old 12x12 egg cartons. They were meant to be a great form of soundproofing but, in my opinion, that was bullshit. They were useless, and all the neighbours hated me with all my noise, or, as they would say, 'racket'.

With drumming, it's alright teaching yourself the basics, but it's far better to get help and some form of tuition to learn the basic rhythms. As a mate of mine once said to me, "If I give you a fish, you eat for a meal, if I give you a rod, you eat for life". Not that that's got anything to do with drumming. The lessons, though not cheap, were a great help. The initial outlay came back to me tenfold in the years ahead. I had various lessons and can honestly say it was money well spent.

My first teacher was Jerry Harris from Bowker Vale. It cost £3 for half an hour, and was a round trip walk of five or six miles. In 1974/75, that was a lot of dollars… AND A VERY LONG WALK.

The lessons were in Jerry's little studio, which was set up in a box room. He used to teach me rhythms and we would play along to songs from the charts.

The Jerry Harris Drum Tape.

To this day, I still have the cassette with all the songs I used to play along to!

Mississippi by Pussycat… Tavares and *Don't Take Away The Music*, and *We've Only Just Begun*, by The Carpenters to name just a few.

The tape still has the voice of the top 40 presenter at the time, Mr Tom Brown. Amazing. Just hearing that voice provokes so many great memories.

I then went on to have a few lessons from a rudimental drummer called George, who lived in Weaste. He was a different style of drummer. He was all about rolls and rudiments, and it was boring as fuck, if I'm honest. Paradiddles, rolls and triplets… So, that didn't last long. No offence, George.

I had aspirations of being the next top drummer who'd be heading to the bright lights of London to seek my fame and fortune. The only problem with that little fact was that I wasn't good enough. Nor would I ever be. To be the best and top of your game, you have to be focussed, and you must practice and rehearse like there's no tomorrow.

I was, and always would remain, an average drummer.

I remember a guy who lived in our street. He was a drummer who was well into rock, by the name of Cyril Oxton. He used to practice on his drum pad in the spare room and, although he was good on the pad, I had my reservations that he could produce the same quality on the major drum kit.

Also, my next-door neighbour, Mark Clarke who was a Boys Brigade drummer practiced and had the 'mama dadda 2 stroke roll' off to a tee, but that's all he could do. He couldn't play the full kit, which gives insight into the fact there are different types of drummers.

I knew that if I wanted to get to the top I'd have to be better and would have to practice more than those guys, but I didn't.

As for the bright lights, don't ask me… but why is it that every kid thinks the bright lights of London are where you go to seek success. After all, the lights there are no different than anywhere else.

I can't recall the exact details of how, what, when, where or why, but I joined a group in school. It had Mark Reid and Leslie Ong on guitars, though I had no idea who was the singer, bass and keyboard players, or if at all we had any. But then, after speaking to the mine of information, Mr Les Ong, I was informed that the other members of our school band were Steve Boardman on vocals, Graham Francis on guitar, and a guy called Trevor Ryder. Oh, the joys of being young.

No offence to those guys, but I don't recall them, and wouldn't know them if I fell over them. Thinking about it, Les Ong could quite honestly be pulling my pants down there with that bit of knowledge.

Anyway, we did two gigs. The first was at Hope Church disco in August 1977, and the second at the Boniface's youth club in Lower Broughton. That was where all the local dickheads wanted to beat us up, just because we were in a band and they couldn't play an instrument. Oh, and apparently all the girls liked us as well.

I can laugh now. Jealous fuckers, eh! And nothing's changed forty years later.

I've recently learned from Mr Leslie Ong that some of the songs we covered were *Hotel California*, *Caroline* by Status Quo, and *Hey Rock n Roll* by the good old

Showaddywaddy.

After leaving school, I began playing in social clubs alongside a keyboard player. We backed cabaret artistes, and occasionally I would play alongside a pianist. Boy, did I want to slash my wrists. I think I did almost two years in various clubs while also rehearsing with a rock band. They were two lads from Salford Precinct, and Phil Lindley from Kingsley Avenue, Lower Kersal. He was a long-haired rocker who had a big church-style organ in his spare room. We rehearsed, but never did a gig. I've no idea why, but one thing I do remember was about two guys, Jimmy and Nobby Clarke from Shirley Avenue. Because I didn't drive, they used to cart my drums around in their three-wheeler car. They were like a pair of Del Boys, but let me just say that I was ever so grateful. Cheers, boys.

THE CLARKEYS

My second drum kit was black. I re-covered it in an orange wrap outside my dad's shed.

The Phil Lindley Rock Band.

Still the Lindley Rock Band.

I persevered during the daytime doing my joinery apprenticeship with Shepherd Construction through the week. The weekends were filled with playing drums in the social clubs backing cabaret artistes. By the way, this was a priceless experience and put me in good standing for what was about to happen.

Northumberland Street Conservative Club in Salford.

While drumming doing cabaret at various clubs around Manchester (I used to get these gigs from an agent in Bury called Dave Lee), I got a phone call from Jerry Harris, my old drum teacher.

He asked me if I wanted to join a working cabaret band. I said, "Are you having a laugh? Too right, I do!".

Jerry had received a call from a certain Mervin Walker, a singer/entertainer from Leigh, also known as Gary de Paul. He was a singer with a cabaret act and backing band, and they were in need of a new drummer. Theirs was either leaving or about to be axed. I made the call and went to meet them the following Friday night at Oldham Athletic Football Club.

I watched the band and joined there and then. Within a week, I was travelling up and down the country doing cabaret for £5 a gig. The money wasn't the issue. The truth was, I would have done it for free, even though as a backing drummer I usually got around £18 less commission.

So, I was an apprentice joiner during the day and at night I was a travelling wilbury, up and down the country.

I gigged everywhere. We went to places like Stoke, Liverpool, Sunderland etc. Me on the drums, Big Mike on guitar, and Paul Walker (Merv's son) on the organ and playing bass on the organ's pedals (clever bastard). The act was no Rolling Stones, but I was enjoying all aspects of the travelling, the gigs, and on occasions, the females. Mmmm.

There was a strange side to the travelling home through the night bit. While all and sundry were tucked up in there beddy-bo-byes, we were often stopping off at the motorway services to have some scran. It's quite a weird feeling that is still with me today – the thought that the world keeps going on and there's activity happening while most people are fast asleep in bed.

As we ventured up and down the country, a friend of mine used to come with us quite a bit. He was getting a taste of the bug. He kind of struck up a friendship with Paul, the keyboard player, who convinced him to learn the bass guitar. It would then allow him to ditch the club organs and play on a keyboard instead. Gary de Paul, the main man in the band, had visions of turning his act into the next Grumbleweeds or Black Onyx. He wanted us all to come off our instruments and participate in sketches.

At first, I said "Fuck that, I'm a drummer and I'm staying put", but he convinced me otherwise, and that was it, my new comedic apprenticeship kicked into gear. Over the next year or two, by watching all other acts, we were able to develop the group into the Gary de Paul Showband.

We all became an essential part of the setup, instead of just being a backing group.

Gary De Paul Showgroup

Along the way, another friend of ours called Jimmy Carroll, (*not* the comedian) replaced Big Mike on guitar. And then we brought in Merv's friend, Phil, to work the lights.

He even bought his own lights, bless the lad.

Gary de Paul band with two additional members, Jim and Phil.

AND SO A COMEDIAN WAS BORN

At first, my comedy consisted of a dressed-up schoolboy emerging from the back of the club looking for his mother! Then I moved onto Andy Pandy, Max Wall, and the impression I did of the rugby guy, Eddie Waring. Ah, well…

Me dressed as a schoolboy. I'd lost me mam.

At this point we (that's all of us other than Gary de Paul), were still on £5 a gig. By that point, we weren't happy about it.

After all, we were all the act and not just musicians any more. So, we held a meeting and demanded that the fee for the

ALLAN BIRKIN

gig be split five ways after costs. The boss tried to convince us we would be no better off. Yeah, right. In essence, his livelihood was now being threatened, so he tried his best to convince us that because of fuel, agents' fees, his cig and beer money and the fact he had a mortgage, it wouldn't work. Ha ha.

He had no choice but to agree. Our money trebled overnight, but that signed the death knell and the group lasted a fortnight. He left, taking with him his trusted son to start over again. Me,

Oxo and Jim just recruited a singer, Les from Portsmouth, and a keyboards player, Brian from Swinton.

We started our own act called Spottymolldoon, a comedy showband that soon established itself on the cabaret circuit. This was like my third apprenticeship. I was mostly responsible for the running of the band, from obtaining the gigs to organising and playing the drums while developing my comedy on the stage.

We also recruited Jim's brother, Anthony, to do the lights.

While all the other members had an eye for comedy, they weren't as keen as I was for doing all the research. To take things forward, I spent hours and £s going to see other acts that were similar, so we could take a little sketch here and another sketch there. By watching what worked for others, and seeing the ideas that took them years to perfect, we could take the gags and use them in weeks. Hard graft will always bring results but you only get out of life what you put in. All my hard work would pay off for me in the long run.

In the early days of putting this band together, we didn't earn enough money to make a living, and several band members (including myself) didn't hold down a full-time job. This meant signing on the good old rock n roll – the DOLE!!

One contracts agent we worked for came back to bite us on the arse because he shopped us to the dole when we refused to pay him commission for future work. We felt he didn't do anything for it. I've spoken before about people in glass houses… but, let me tell you about this guy! In fact, don't get me started on that one, or I'll be here all day.

Our typical contract from the arsehole!!

MISSED THE BOAT

.... SPOTTYMOLLDOON ....

With reference to your above artiste(s) contract with us for the period commencing
and ending   , we detail hereunder a list of venues pre

DATE	VENUE	CHECK-IN TIME
Fri 28 Jan	Jubilee Social Centre Club, Highcliffe, Spittal, Berwick On Tweed	7.00 pm
Sat 29 Jan	Dumfries Labour Club, Lochside Road, Dumfries	7.00 pm
Sun 30 Jan aft	Cowdenbeath Miners' Club, Broad Street, Cowdenbeath	1.00 pm
Sun 30 Jan eve	Cowie Miners' Welfare, Pitt Street, Cowie	7.00 pm
Mon 31 Jan	PRESENTLY VACANT — TELEPHONE OFFICE ✳	
Tue 1 Feb	The Lion Club, HMS Cochrane, Rosyth, Fife	5.00 FOR 7.00 SOUND
Wed 2 Feb	The Trident Club, HMS Neptune, Faslane, Helensburgh	5.00 FOR 7.00 SOUND
Thur 3 Feb	PRESENTLY VACANT — TELEPHONE OFFICE ✳	
Fri 4 Feb	PRESENTLY VACANT — TELEPHONE OFFICE ✳	
Sat 5 Feb	The CDC Club, Town Centre, Cumbernauld	7.00 pm
Sun 6 Feb aft	~~XXXXXXXXXXXXXXXXXXXXXXXXXXXXXX~~ Crosshill Social Club, Crosshill, Lochgelly	1.00 pm
Sun 6 Feb eve	PRESENTLY VACANT — TELEPHONE OFFICE ✳	

WHITBURN MINERS,
LOTHIAN

The above list is for the information and guidance of artistes but it must be understood that, while the details of pick-ups are correct at the time of writing, the list is subject to alteration. It is important that artistes remain in touch with the office during the period of their Contract in order that they may be kept informed of any alterations, additions or cancellations of bookings.
Where the above list shows a number of venues in excess of the minimum number of shows guaranteed in the original must be stressed that this does not necessarily imply that an additional number of shows will ultimately be fulfilled.

One of the ten day runs which he booked us on that we in turn refused to pay him the commission for.

Our refusal to pay culminated in...

Pop agent shops Spotty Muldoon

POP group agent Roy Mozley shopped a group to the DHSS after a dispute over his fee, Eccles Magistrates heard.

As a result the three members of "Spotty Muldoon" were fined for making false statements to obtain benefits.

They were James Andrew Carroll, of Carlton Road, Salford, Alan David Birkin, of Cedar Place, Lower Broughton; and Alan Oxton, of South Radford Street, Salford.

Mr Edward Donnelly, for the DHSS, said the money ran into hundreds rather than thousands of pounds.

Mr Simon Nicholl, defending, said they started a group for their own amusement about three years ago.

They were then in employment and there was no question of their claiming benefit.

Bookings increased and they came into contact with Mr Mozley, an agent for pop groups.

"He led them to believe that, if they went under his wing, they would be able to make a full-time job of it."

Mr Mozley got them some bookings, some of them quite far afield. But he did not live up to their expectations, although he was taking a substantial fee.

Mr Mozley knew they were claiming benefit but did nothing about it until they had a dispute with him about the large fee he was taking and the service they were getting for it.

He then reported them to the DHSS, declared Mr Nicholl.

"I say that by way of explanation," he told the magistrates.

He added that, August last year, the ban received £850, but out of that had to come the co of equipment, travel an keep for abut three weeks.

Each was fined £50, an Carroll and Birkin wer also given conditional di charges for six months.

MP feeds patient

THE Eccles MP helped to feed a fellow-patient in hospital recently because the nurses were so busy.

Mr Lewis Carter-Jones, who was in St Thomas's Hospital in London for a check-up, told the Journal: "The nurses were being flogged to death. I don't know how they coped. They were being slave-driven."

At a particularly busy time the MP saw that a man on the other side of the ward was having difficulty with his meal.

"I just went across and offered to help — I cut up his meat for him," he said.

At the latest meeting of Eccles Constituency Labour Party he added: "The cutbacks mean the weak in society are carrying the burden and decent men and women are compelled to take action they don't want to."

Man caught

POLICE have caught the man who stole disco equipment from Monton Methodist Youth Club last month.

Michael Henry Manning, aged 21, of First Avenue, Swinton, admitted to Eccles Magistrates that he stole equipment and records worth £1,200.

Mr John Barguss, prosecuting, said that your leader Mr Huddlesto went to the club at 5.3 p.m. on Sept. 23.

"He left some of th small windows open t keep the premises aire and he found a larg quantity of disco equip ment and records ha been taken."

Property worth £85 had been found in Manning's bedroom, leaving balance of £35 outstanding.

He recommended th

Wounding charge

AN ECCLES man was sent by magistrates to Manchester Crown Court for trial on a wounding charge.

Geoffrey Grange, aged 20, of Cecil Road, is alleged to have wounded Gareth Trevor Hughes in the Packet

The band ran for four years and definitely took its toll on our friendships. Living in each other's pockets meant we grew apart and the dislike for each other became intolerable. Over that four-year period, we worked lots of gigs in lots of areas. We even went through several line-up changes, we lost the lights man, and then we realised our keyboard player was an actual WALLY and was in fact the brakes on our system. By losing him and replacing what he did on guitar, the band actually worked a lot better, and we had a little more cash as well. Sowwee Bwian.

Spottymolldoon. At this stage, down to a four-piece.

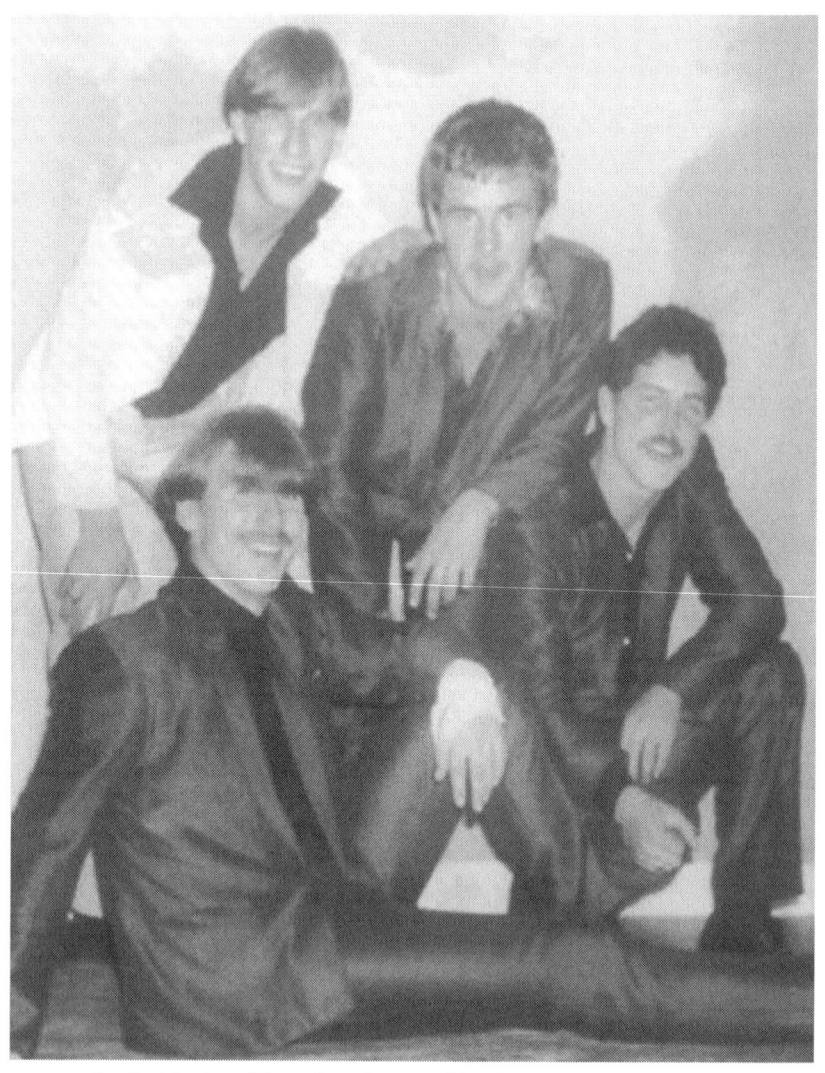

Our final Spottymolldoon photo. Spottymolldoon's act can be found on YouTube.

Because we were together a lot the tensions grew and grew. I couldn't take it any longer and I opted to leave, but I was convinced to stay. So, the guitarist decided to leave instead. He left and we paid him out for his share of whatever assets the band had. At first, it gave us a new lease of life, but that lasted for all of ten minutes. The truth was that it was only masking the real problem – I didn't like being with that lot anymore and I really, truly wanted out. I wanted to become a front man. I wanted to sing too. There was an occasion when I tried to, but others were having none of it. I never knew the real reason, but I knew I had the potential to go it alone.

We even tried changing the band's name. This was just another form of a new lease of life. We decided on just doing music and no comedy. We changed the name to The M.O.T. Band, which meant venues weren't expecting comedy, just something a little different. But whatever we did was still of no use. I had run my course and that meant there was only one option. I made my decision and there was no changing my mind. I was getting out and decided on doing it sooner rather than later.

THE M.O.T. BAND

THE M.O.T. BAND

We had some good times with the band, and some bad ones too. But, like life itself, it's all part of the process. When we were in this band, as in the one before, we all thought we were the dog's bollocks. We were going to be stars, but we were just another act. Nothing more, nothing less.

I finally decided this band wasn't for me any longer, so we found a replacement, trained him up and he was almost ready to replace me when he had to be thrown in at the deep end. All of a sudden, I left.

It was on Friday May 24th 1984.

It was the very day when my dad passed away.

James Frank Parkin, my dad. God bless him.

We were doing a two-nighter at the Novotel in Bradford, so my gear was all set up. In at the deep end he went and I was gone. I don't think the other members actually realised how much work I put in, but they soon found out.

I did actually work with the ex-band one night at The Paddock in Salford. They supported me on a door show that I had put on. The band ceased to exist soon after that, while I went on from strength to strength. The singer, Les Budd, also went solo and I worked with him too.

Of all the memories that stuck with me from the Spottymolldoon days, the biggest was the theft of my Premier poly silver drum kit. I worked like a dog to buy it from Mamelok on Deansgate. It was not the cheapest of music shops. All in all, with the drums, Trilok stands and Avedis Zylgyian cymbals, it set me back a fortune. It cost me almost £2500, and in the early 80s, that was a Football Pools win.

My Premier drum kit, in poly silver.

I wasn't the only member to lose his equipment. The whole van was taken from outside my house in Lower Broughton, and it was probably a well-planned operation rather than a spur of the moment thing. Everybody lost everything. The van was found three days later, empty in Cheetham Hill.

The final Spottymolldoon line up. Only Alan Oxton remained from the days of Gary de Paul. Funny how things work out.

Not one to rest on my laurels, I joined another band three days later. They were called The Paul Rivers Band. Yes, I was just on the drums and was back doing clubs up and down the country again, but I knew this was just the stepping stone needed for my entrance as a solo performer. As well as doing the groups for the last five or six years, I was also doing a little TV work. Mostly I was an extra, but I did get two little breaks where I thought, "This is going to get me to the big time". Not a chance!

I did an advert for Jewson's (the builders), and, guess what, they cut me out. Then I did three episodes of *Emmerdale Farm*. Wahey, I was in the big time, or so I thought. I thought I could do it, but the truth is that acting isn't as easy as it looks. My biggest line in *Emmerdale Farm* ended up on the cutting room floor as well.

I actually used Spottymolldoon as a name just in case I did get somewhere. I thought I'd be able to promote the band as well.

So, I had a spell with The Paul Rivers Band, while I went along to talent show after talent show, not to win but just to gain experience. After all, being a singer without a voice was basically having to start all over again.

In fairness it wasn't happening quickly enough, so I put my own band together and called us Jade.

Jade was a four-piece band and I was free to sing to my heart's content. I chose the majority of the songs and handpicked the band members, as well as the songs. I was also free to tell all the gags I wanted. In the short period the band existed, we managed (after several rehearsals) to be the Chris Quentin backing band, doing Salford, Leicester and Blackpool. Chris Quentin was the *Coronation Street* star, Brian Tyldesley.

A year and a half after starting the band, doing pub after pub and club after club, I'd got what I needed out of it. I'd become enabled to stand on my own as a stand-up comic, so I was off.

SCULLY: My first solo stand-up gig was a spot on a Sunday afternoon show for gents, run by John Robinson Junior, who was a very well-established comedian. It featured a host of female strippers and was at the Belle Vue Lake Hotel on Hyde Road in Belle Vue, Manchester. Apparently, they had Sunday afternoon stag shows quite regularly.

I bounced on the stage full of confidence and held my own, performing under the name of Scully.

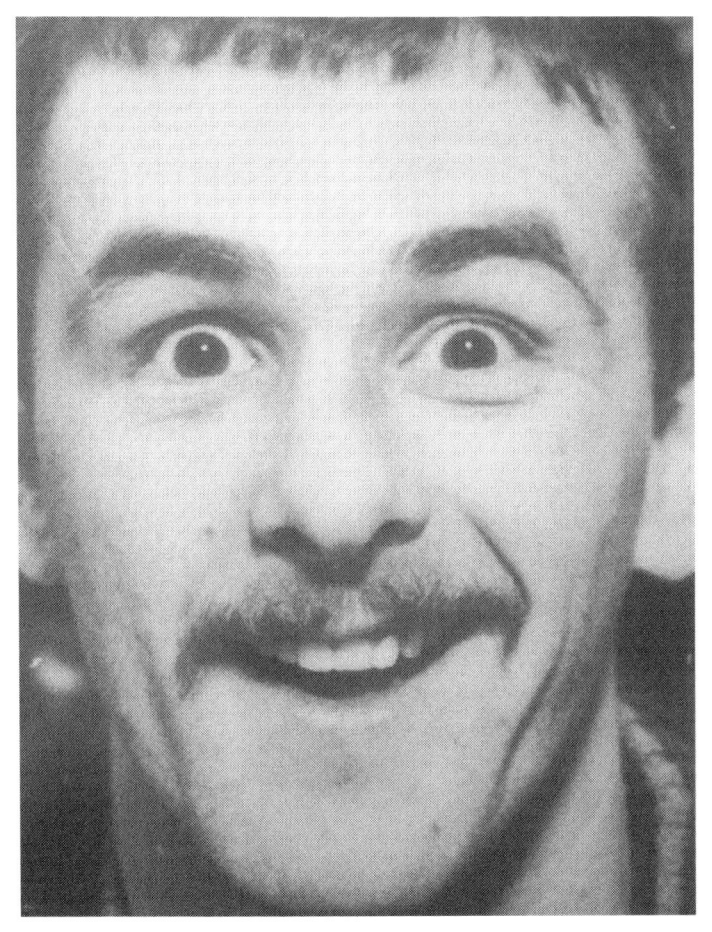

Scully!

So, that's how it all started. To go from drummer to singer to stand-up comedian means a lot happened in between. A very lot. But if I ramble on too much the whole book would be on how it all started. Maybe one day I will come back to it and tell you more.

When it comes to doing gigs, there's basically a pecking order. You start off doing pubs and clubs, gaining the experience to launch you into better venues and better gigs, nightclubs and theatres. The pubs and clubs are basically your apprenticeship culminating in the better venues and more money. Not all acts progress beyond the pub and club scene, forever staying as a work in progress, though it doesn't stop them from earning a living.

It just means that they never progress to the better venues that pay the top dollar. As a performer or act hones their craft, they might gain a little exposure by TV or radio. This boosts their audience, and, in turn, money. This type of work eventually leads to putting bums on seats.

When I launched my solo career, I made a quick decision to have a blue act. Becoming a blue comedian was a good thing in one way but a bad decision in another. By being blue, you limit the places you can work, although, when I was doing it, there were still many venues to keep me going. On the plus side, being an act of this nature very quickly gained me a little notoriety doing the clubs. If I'd been a squeaky-clean comic, I would still be doing the rounds today. The opportunities and openings for acts to make it on television is very limited and it's not what you know in this business but who.

Several of the top agents have those slots all sewn up, so unless you're on their books you can forget it.

I did make it to the top of the bill slot, but I never had the chance to appear on TV as a comic. I just settled for the live work. Even though I worked the bigger venues, I was there as part of a show. It wasn't the case that people paid £10 a ticket to see only me. The Lakeside, The Willows and The Talk of the North etc, were some of the venues I did under those terms. I did The Pavilion Theatre in Glasgow as part of the strip-r-oke tour which was good but didn't quite go to plan.

I also worked Benidorm on three occasions for a week at a time. I was topping the bill, but that's no mean feat (everybody did ha ha), and, besides that, the majority of the crowd still didn't know their top of the bill act.

As well as treading the boards over the coming years I tried all sorts of other acts to keep me both varied, and to improve my talents, from singing to drumming to stripping. I worked on an Elvis tribute and though I spent a fortune on the backing tracks, the stage wear, and rehearsed the whole show, I never once did it live. Elvis just never left the building.

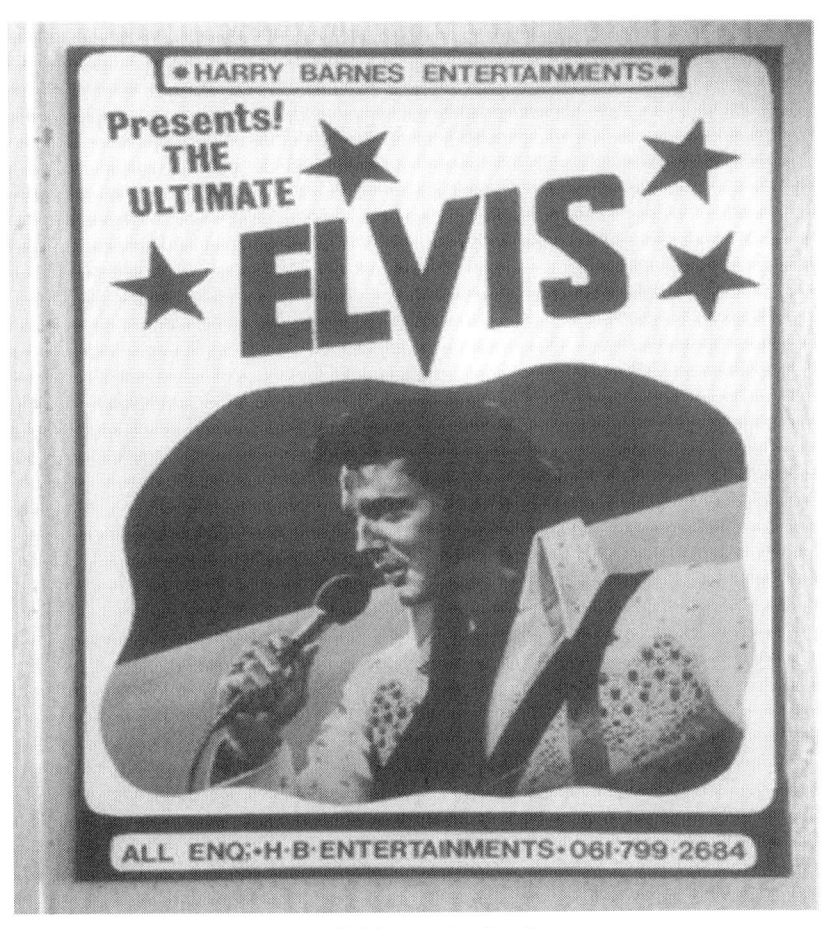

"A Wannuss, Hee Arrrr"

I also worked on a drumming act similar to the Eric Delaney show, but with just one man. That too, never left the rehearsal room, though, believe it or not, I'm still toying with it to this very day, and I've just learnt *Dance With The Devil* by Cozy Powell..

I'm also working on my own song with a vague similarity to *Let There Be Drums*, the track by Sandy Nelson, one of the 1960s drumming sensations…

The Bleeding Noisy Drum Show never quite got going, but it is still a work in progress and you just never know… it's not over till the fat lady sings. Yahaaaaaaaaaaaa.

MISSED THE BOAT

My drum kit in 2016. Premier with great cymbals and acquired for a song. Not like in the old days when everything cost a fortune. As they say in life

"Knowledge is power".

I then did the Bay City Rollers tribute. (see later in the book). It took me long enough, but I did get that to the gigging stage. I started with the *Full Monty* lads (again, see later in the book) as the backing singers, going on to replace the four lads with two girls, Samia and Jemma. Then I went solo to do a final couple of shows in 2016 with a few novices who were more than happy to get up there and let rip, shangalanging. After me and the girls had a spell as an Abba tribute as well, Jemma decided to go solo so we set off as a duo for a short while, in fact till Jemma's confidence was high enough for her to go solo, then off she went too.

3
OPPORTUNITY KNOCKED

I WAS NOW FAIRLY ESTABLISHED ON THE CLUB CIRcuit as a stand-up comedian, although my venues were limited because I chose the route of being blue. There was lots of swearing, telling naughty jokes, and taking the mickey. I think I chose blue because of a mixture of two things. Firstly, I felt being a cheeky chappie worked for my personality. Second, (and probably most important at the time) was if I didn't have an act that was a crowd puller and stayed lily-white, I would probably have been doing the same mundane work for a decade or so.

But this way, I built a name very quickly, and, after all, it worked well for the likes of Bernard Manning, Chubby Brown and the now-extinct Jackie Carlton. Also, although I never saw the great Al Showman work, I heard him a few times on tape. This just names a few of my inspirations, so I thought, "Why not?"

I most certainly could hold my own when it came to entertaining a live audience, but my act was definitely a no-no for television. In this day and age, most comics swear on television, but times have changed. So, I'd just do my gig, get my money then chalk it down as another one done and only 61,000 more gigs to go. Ha ha, that's just a joke.

It was all well and good earning a living, but (like most entertainers), the goal was to get to better gigs that paid more money, and the only way to do that was to build up your name so that you became an attraction that put bums on seats. TV was the biggest outlet to do just that, but to get that break, you needed a lot more than just a good act. You needed a lot of luck, and to be in the right place at the right time. And, the biggest deal breaker of them all (and, believe you me, the most important) - it wasn't what you knew, but who.

Over the years, I made several attempts to climb the ladder. Although my act wasn't original, it was an act people would pay good money to see.

I was a clubland comic, but was pretty sure that, with the right breaks, I could have gone on to bigger and better things. I mean, let's have it right, I was doing the same gigs for the same money as the likes of Lee Evans and Billy Pearce, and even the then almost-ancient, Johnnie Casson!

Touring the land's clubs and pubs to build up your name would have taken not just my lifetime but yours and your best mate's mates too.

Basically, the task was an impossible one. TV and the media enable entertainment at the flick of a switch and the power of the media is immense, but getting in is so ridiculously hard.

There were several routes to the masses, depending on which category you fell into. If you were a singer or group, then your outlet was a record deal, *Top of the Pops*, and the radio. For cabaret acts, it was the likes of *Opportunity Knocks*, *The Comedians*, and *Sunday Night at the London Palladium*. Again, getting on such shows was like finding a block of gold with a metal detector.

To actually get onto a show you could be one of two things, brilliant or crap, but still you needed the luck. Even though my act wasn't right for television in its format of being a cross between Chubby and Bernard, I could have changed it a little for the small screen and saved the blue humour for live. This is what a lot of comics such as Bob Monkhouse and Jim Davidson did. When I say that my act was a cross between Manning and Chubby, this is how I saw those two guys. Manning was a joke-telling piss-taker, where Chubby did one-liner after one-liner with the odd song and long gag chucked in. He was one hell of a machine with the lines and didn't take the piss unless called upon, but could repel a heckler with some fantastic heckler repellents. I'm not calling either Bernard or Chubby, because, thanks to them, I combined both, and put bread on the table.

As it happened, I shared the bill with Big Bernard on a couple of occasions, and his line was "You've just watched the apprentice. Now watch the professional do it". Ha ha, funny fat bastard, our Bernard. Chubby, on the other hand, fell out with me for using his gags. I can understand him being a little riled, but, in all fairness, I was never in a million years a threat to his livelihood.

I can hear you now – "Well, tell us then". OK, here's how it happened. I was working Redcar, near to Middlesborough, one Saturday night. The following day I had another gig, also somewhere up the north east, so I decided to stay the night. Redcar was Chubby's home town and, when I got chatting to the concert secretary of the club, it turned out that he was Chubby Brown's mate. He told me where he lived, so the next day, as brazen as you like, I knocked on Chubby's door. These days, you wouldn't even get through the gates, but I'm talking the late 1980s.

What a man. He was a true gentleman and scholar. He invited me in, made me a cuppa and spared me a good half hour of his time while we chatted in his shed. That was where the master worked his magic almost every day. I honestly can't say a bad word about him. From day one, I've admired his work ethic and his act. But, most of all, from that day alone, I admired the generosity he showed me – a complete stranger. The next time I met him he was working Fagin's, a night club situated in the city centre of Manchester. One of our fellow comics, John Robinson

Junior was compere, and politely told Chubby that I was using all his gags. It was not necessarily true, but I was using some. Let's have it right though, his gags were superb and the venues I was working would not have made an ha'porth of difference, but still I could understand his not liking .

Although I apologised, I have no regrets. So, it came to the next time Chubby was performing in Manchester at The Talk of The North in Eccles. It was a sit-down-meal type of venue and I had booked for a meal with Harry Barnes and another fellow comic, Mike Lancaster. I was probably being cocky to Harry and Mike, letting them know that I knew Chubby. I should have just enjoyed the night in silence. I went to the dressing room where I was met by Chubby's minders who informed me I wasn't welcome. In fact, I wasn't welcome in the venue and I was asked to leave before Chubby hit the stage to perform. I left without causing a fuss because I didn't want to ruin it for my friends. I will tell you though, and I'm not embarrassed to admit it, I listened to the whole show at the back door. Yes, in the pissing-down rain ha ha.

Just like me, there were many comics who were good at their job, funny, professional and yet also couldn't catch that break. Jimmy Carol, Mike Cash, Max Pressure, Frankie Allen, Dave Baron, Buzzer Jones, Ned Kelly and Bobby Bender, to name but a few.

But I was young and ambitious and ready to be the next king of comedy. *Opportunity Knocks*, the main big television talent show was holding auditions in Wythenshawe for their forthcoming series. I knew my act would be too blue for Hughie Green's talent scouts, so I worked a little harder to cut out the swearing and put in what I thought was a half-decent performance. Looking back, it was probably shite. In fact, it must have been shite because I didn't get on the show, but a 150-year women playing spoons on a kitchen sink did!! I reckon her lips were getting locked around someone's todger, ha ha.

Anyhow, it wouldn't have mattered how good my act was on the day, the aftermath saw to it that my act only made the cutting room floor. Some southerner who was working as a runner for the programme, decided to single me out as a talker disrupting the show and ordered me to leave the room. I was young and cocky and thought "Who does she think she is talking to?", and gave her both barrels in front of everyone, the crowd and the TV people. Safe to say, my opportunity was well and truly knocked.

Perhaps my cocky, know-it-all attitude was going to be my downfall. There was no doubt when booked to entertain with microphone in hand I was in the top percentage, but when it came to being an arse-licker, I was well and truly at the bottom.

I got another chance to escape the working men's club circuit. TV producers were looking for the next Freddie Starr or Russ Abbot, so I headed to the Oldham Coliseum on a cold, wet and windy Sunday evening. The auditorium was full with almost 1200 people. Wow! I'd never played to such a big crowd. I was in my element working to such a large audience. It takes some doing, but I passed with flying colours.

On the same bill was Shane Ritchie, fresh from his stint as a Butlin's redcoat. Clever lad, he went on stage, played to the TV producers with nicey-nicey gags and died a death with the audience. But, the men who counted most loved him. Me, old clever bollocks, played to the crowd and brought the house down. But the stuck-up TV men, the ones who counted, never even bothered to write down my name, and, as they say, the rest is history. Look at Shane Ritchie now… he who laughs last, eh?

So, it was back to my life on the road, travelling up and down the motorway, storming the gigs and selling a few tapes. But, the next morning, as normal, you were well and truly forgotten. But, on the plus side, it was still better than doing a normal nine to five job. Taken in those terms, my employment was ace!

But, like all jobs, the glamour can soon disappear. Being on the road can get a little tedious, boring and lonely… spending two or three hours driving to a venue, setting up your gear, performing, then dropping all the gear, packing up and doing the long drive back home. Aargggh. Wouldn't it be great if you could walk out of your front door straight onto stage, perform then walk off stage and straight through your own front door? That would be bliss. Life would have been ten times easier if the audiences I was performing to were there to see me and paid at the door. But, without TV or media, I was destined to stay treading the boards. Ah well, so be it. Then, right out of the blue, what do you know? I got another chance. It could have been the big chance I'd waited for. In the early 70s, a Granada TV producer called Johnny Hamp took a group of clubland comics, put them on a weekly show called *The Comedians*, and made them all household names. Their work went through the roof. They got better gigs and mega money. The power of TV. We were in the 90s, and Granada (via Sky) looked set to do the same, launching a show called *The New Comedians*, a six-week pilot show that could well have launched a brand new set of comedians on the showbiz world. Me and a good friend, Buzzer Jones, were given a chance. We set of for The Witchwood in Ashton. The producer wasn't Johnny Hamp, but a clubland comic himself called Buzz Hawkins. His chum (and the compere linking the whole show) was Dave Buck, a guy I had known a long time, yet, as it turned out, I didn't know him at all. His instructions to me and Buzzer (a pair of blue clubland comics) was "Keep it clean".

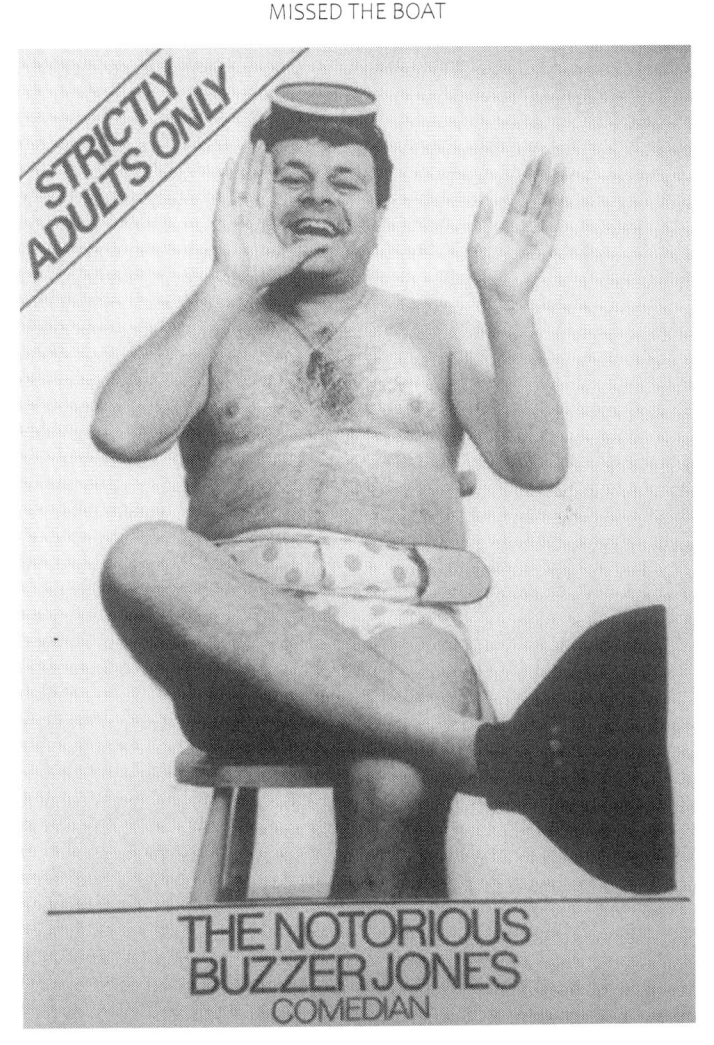

My old mucka Buzzer Jones.

We did it, but struggled to perform to our best. It's not easy when you have to watch your p's and q's while trying to entertain a live audience. On top of that, the cameras were glaring at us, scrutinising our every word. It wasn't easy, even for polished performers such as us two. So, it was done and, as we showbiz luvvies like to say, "It was in the can". All we had to do was sit and wait, let the programme air and see if we were going to have any impact.

The worst bit was telling all my friends, associates and family that I was going to be on *The New Comedians*, only to be (as I put it), stabbed in the back. Not only by the producer, but by a guy I thought I knew, and whose words were "Keep it clean". It was terrible watching the programme air week after week with gags from every other comic but me and Buzzer. To put it nicely, the icing on the cake was performed week in week out by the compere whose language and humour were far from clean.

What a pair of bastards. They do say "What goes around, comes around", "Karma's a bitch", and "Everything comes to those who wait". Well, I couldn't wait, so I picked up the phone and with both barrels they got it, full belt. Ringing Granada, I wanted to have it out with the producer. His words were, "We couldn't fit you in".

Fit us in?! The air was blue… not one fuckin gag… you fuckin pair of tossers.

I suppose in hindsight, I should have just done my act as it was. Better still, I shouldn't have gone at all. We were lambs to the slaughter. Lambs, that's what we were, fuckin baaaaaaaaaaaaaaaaaaaaa.

It's not very often I credit myself with anything, but I will with this little one. I had no chance of getting on TV, so another

BUZZER JONES

The gurning Buzzer Jones.

route was through video. Get one out, push it and get to a bigger audience without having to trek the globe. I contacted a guy called Darren Kinnersley Hill at PolyGram. I managed to persuade him to come and watch me work, and he travelled up from London to Fleetwood. I felt I performed well, and although he was impressed, he also realised he would have a job shifting enough units to make any money. Because, outside of that venue, that evening, nobody knew who I was. I was an unknown and he would be lucky to shift five without spending a fortune on marketing. His words were, "We need a blue comic with a big following that will shift sales without spending a fortune". I then said, because I'm not malicious, "There's only one blue comic capable of doing that, but I'm sure he would be reluctant to put his act out there for all to see. It would be Chubby Brown". "Chubby who?" he said. "Roy Chubby Brown," I said. "He's from the north east. He's brilliant and has already got a massive following and is filling venues all over the country. Without a doubt, he's the best, by far".

Enough said. PolyGram offered Roy Chubby Brown a big, fat cheque, and the helmet hit the shelves. OMG, the success was phenomenal, and to this day and 24/25 videos later, he's still doing the business. Nice one, Chubbs. I did go back to Mr Kinnersley one last time with an idea that would have got me the exposure I needed, but, once again, the door got shut. They weren't interested. What's that I hear you say? "What was the idea?" OK, I will tell you. But, to prove I was good at what I'm talking about, in the year 2000 I organised and arranged a school reunion for all the pupils that left Buile Hill High School in 1977. Advertising was expensive, so I concocted a bullshit story that the press bought. And bingo! We got almost half a page. Other papers picked it up and followed suit. The marketing for our school reunion was complete, and a good night was had by all. OK, so I had to dress up like a schoolboy for the photo, but that was a small price to pay.

SO… BACK TO MY IDEA.

Allan's old pals turn down a night of 100 girls

BY NEAL KEELING

ALLAN BIRKIN is looking forward to his school reunion — with 100 women.

For former girl pupils at Baile Hill High, Salford, in the mid 70s are travelling from as far as Australia to roll back the years at a glam-rock party in Swinton . . . but no lads.

Allan, aged 38, of Worsley said: "I have got two adverts in the Manchester Evening News and the response from women has been fantastic. About a hundred are coming but so far not a single lad.

"It's a mystery," said Allan.

"It looks like I am going to have a great time. One woman phoned from Luxembourg, another from Australia, and a third is flying up from Brighton."

"We were all together for five years at Baile Hill and it would be great to see some the boys again too."

The party will be held at Swinton Labour Club in Station Road at 7.30pm on March 31.

A 70s music DJ will be bringing back memories of stars like Shade, Bay City Rollers, and T Rex.

Allan can be contacted on 07968 731654.

■ BACK TO SCHOOL . . . But Allan Birkin wants more old boys to turn up

Me once again generating publicity.

When I approached PolyGram, they said they didn't know how to break me to the masses. I'd given them a few ideas as I thought I had an eye for the odd great one. The picture on the next page shows how easy I could create publicity.

Chubby's initial video sales were in excess of one and two million. PolyGram could have promoted me at the beginning of a Chubby video with a quick one-minute cameo and a sales pitch "This is our next big comic". I would have had a few million minutes of exposure, and boy, that would have helped. But, alas, it just wasn't to be. Kinnersley just dismissed me. He'd found his golden nugget, so, yes you guessed it... that fukker got a piece of my mind as well. Ha ha, yes, I'm a fukka.

"FUCK PolyGram."

In the end, I did release my own videos. The first one was *Putting the F in Laffta*. It was self-financed and recorded at The Jaggy Thistle in Blackpool. It was followed up with a video released through a company called Grosvenor, titled *Who's an Ugly Bastard?* But, like Mr Kinnersley Hill said, "If you're not a name, you won't shift them".

Hence, I have boxfuls of videos and DVDs just gathering dust in my shed at home. Another lesson learnt in the big bad world.

Scully the Bully's *Putting the F in Laffta*.

I decided to do this video which I recorded myself at The Jaggy Thistle in Blackpool, and then had it edited at a friend's studio in North Wales. The video was just for selling at gigs.

Prior to this, I commissioned a company to do me a professional video. I spent over £1000, and I may as well have chucked it down a grid. It was a right pile of shite.

I plodded on regardless, and kept my fingers crossed that I may get lucky and find a company prepared to give me a chance.

A couple of years later, I got a deal for a second video with a company called Grosvenor. It was recorded over two nights at the Chateaux Jacques club in Middleton. The video *bombed*, due to the main two things needed. First of all, a comic's popularity which in my case was pretty zilch, and secondly and the most important, promotion without a large budget and a campaign to back it up. Without that, you are pretty much on a hiding to nothing.

I ended up buying the rights and the stock. I did allow a company to print off 1000 onto DVD. My share still languishes in my new wooden shed.

The Grosvenor UK video release.

> JACK MANAGEMENT IN CONJUNCTION WITH GROSVENOR HOME ENTERTAINMENT LTD.
> Presents
> **THE VIDEO RECORDING OF THE YEAR**
> **SCULLY** THE BULLY IN "LIVE & VERY VERY DANGEROUS"
> You are cordially invited to be part of the audience
> Admission is FREE BUT STRICTLY BY TICKET ONLY on a 1st come 1st served basis
> The Management reserve the right to refuse admission
> at the CHATEAU JACQUES NIGHT CLUB
> Market Place, Middleton, Manchester M24 7AE
> on THURSDAY 25th AUGUST 1994
> Doors open 7 p.m. Show starts 8.30 p.m.
> **THIS SHOW IS STRICTLY LADIES ONLY**
> Featuring **SCULLY** "The North West's most outrageous comedian"
> and **BOY BLUE** "Top Male Exotic Dancer"
> Please arrive as early as possible to be sure of a seat
> ****IF EASILY OFFENDED PLEASE STAY WELL AWAY****

The Recording of *Who's an Ugly Bastard?*

Half the battle of a film's success on release is in the promotion. But, because of the high expense, most companies spend more on the promotion side than the costs incurred in the actual making of the film.

Grosvenor's advertising campaign consisted of what you see here and on the next page. The videos were made available on the shelves at Woolworths, but alongside big names of the day Roy Chubby Brown, Jim Davidson, Jimmy Jones, Billy Connolly etc, whose videos were flying off the shelves. Mine just became the Woollies doorstop for the delivery of everyone else's.

Needless to say, these two adverts passed completely unnoticed. In those days, there was no social media, so it was all cash, cash, budget gone. Scully binned yet again, realising it's not meant to be. Again! Ha ha.

But there's no point
crying over spilt milk.

They do say that God loves a tryer.

While forging a career as a comic, I still longed to sing and play the drums. I put another band together to run alongside my work as a comic.

Scullyduggery, the pop/rock band was good, but while in the rehearsal stages we still saw several members come and go.

A female keyboard player called Jackie Lee Knight, who is sadly no longer with us, was one. Jackie used to be resident at Fagin's in Manchester. Although we never actually performed a live gig with Jackie on the keys, we never got past the rehearsal stage before, she too, decided she wanted a solo career.

We had one of the world's top guitarists in Mr Michael Eaton Dykes, on drums and vocals split with myself we had Mr Nigel Crompton. On bass was Barry, and the new guy on the keys replacing Jackie was Glen, who now resides in sunny Australia.

The band had a little run, and once again, like all other things, it ran its course. I was in and out of all sorts of bands throughout the years, but decided to give drums a miss for a while. It seemed my sticks were destined to be well and truly locked away in the cupboard.

So, as opportunity after opportunity knocked, I began to realise that it wasn't just me, but was a story that runs throughout life. I'm not ashamed to say it, but that little fact is one of my greatest gripes. The fact that another man's future can be placed in the hands of another. Power is a bastard of a thing, especially if it's in the hands of someone whose favourite choice isn't your good self.

Onwards and upwards, as they say…

My Premier drum kit in poly silver.

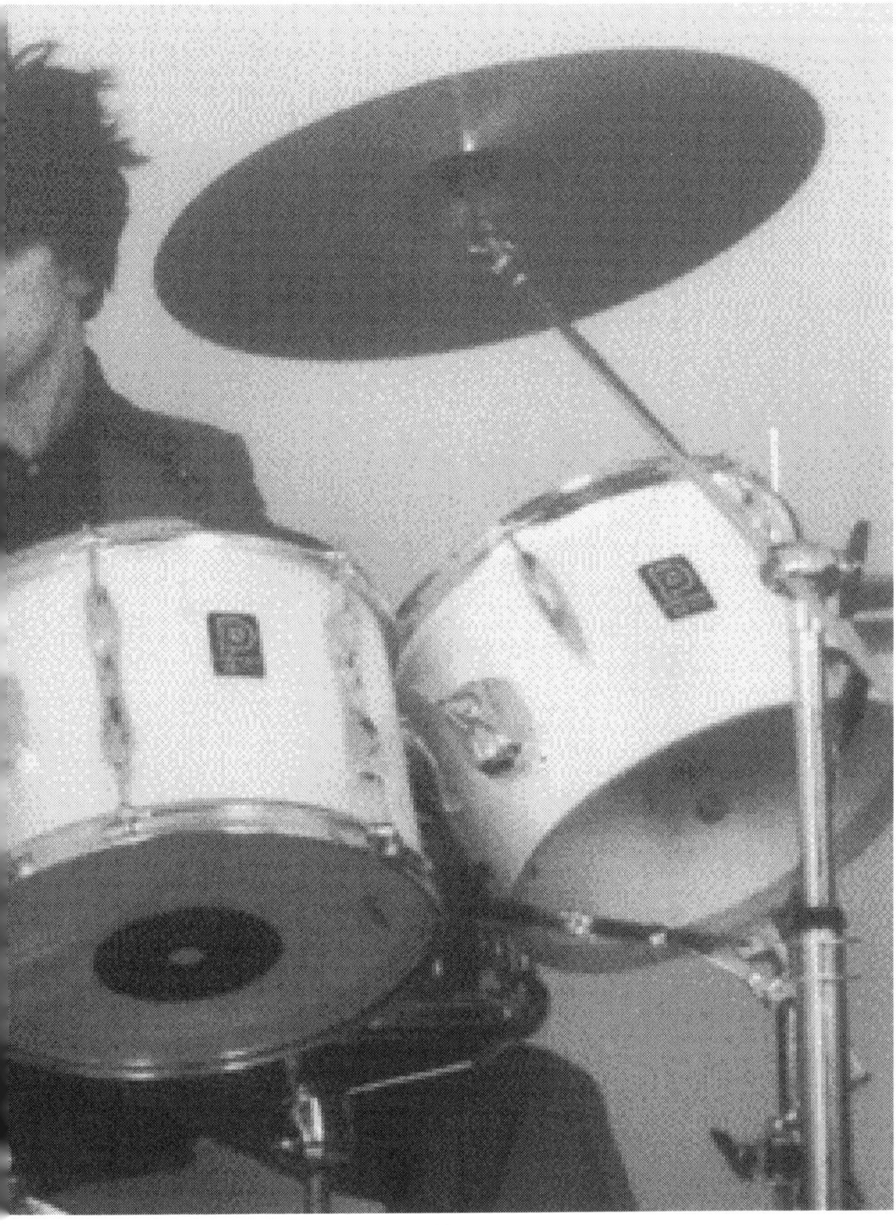

SCULLYDUGGERY

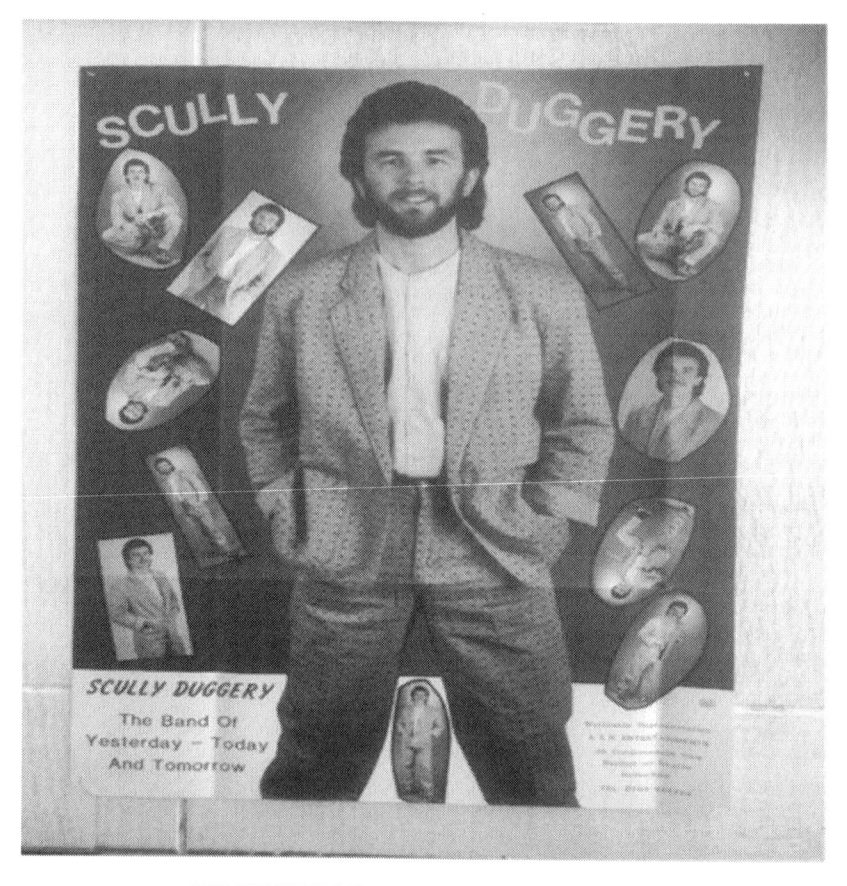

SCULLYDUGGERY! This was the poster to promote the band.

I'm like the werewolf in London.

4
HECKLER, OR DICKHEAD?

AS A COMEDIAN WHO TAKES THE MICKEY OUT OF everyone and anyone at any given moment, learning to deal with people who answer back is part and parcel of the job. Getting heckled is something I thrived on. The fact that I was fairly quick-witted helped an immense amount. It helped that I had a great back-up of ready replies that were tried and tested night after night. They do say there's nothing new in comedy. It's all been done before.

What is new though, is the way it all gets revamped time and again.

I watched many comedians work over the years, mainly to have myself a good laugh, but mostly to see what fantastic lines they used, that I could slightly rearrange and use myself.

I must say that in watching so many comics who invariably used the same lines, I wasn't alone in that fact.

I should imagine there's only a handful of comics who can say, hand on heart, that they were completely original in both the material they used and the jokes that they told.

Not all comedians like being heckled. There are different types of comics. Some just like to tell jokes and not really have the audience's participation, while, for others, it's what they thrive on. It's their bread and butter, so to speak. As a comedian fires his gun, the audience can supply his bullets. As for the audience, a good heckler or hecklers can help push a comic's performance along and help make the show. On the other hand, though, there's the dickheads.

THE DICKHEADS
The not so funny fuckers

My years of experiences have taught me to not only spot the latter, but try my best to steer clear, because, as funny as you are or no matter how fantastic your lines are, you won't win as a comic when faced with the dickhead.

During your performance you get heckled, then you come back with a line or maybe two, and the audience react with laughter. That's when the heckler fades into the background with his humiliation, but occasionally finds the balls or line to retaliate even funnier.

The audience laugh again, bringing him into the comic's act. That's great and all well and good as long as the comic doesn't let the heckler get the better of him, or in fact have the last laugh. And, that's what we term a heckler.

Then there's the dickhead – a person who just constantly shouts out. He doesn't even listen to the lines or punches that the comic is sending his way, and he's oblivious to the humour because he's not even listening to what's going on. The only thing he can hear is his own voice. Such types are to be avoided at all costs. Great lines can be wasted on such non-entities. The dickhead can singlehandedly ruin the comedian's performance, and after all, we're just doing a job that if we don't complete, we run the risk of the venue saying "Sorry lad, we're not paying you for that!" Aaaarghh.

Being a comedian who thrived upon mickey-taking and dealing with hecklers meant I had this air of invincibility about my performance. You need to seem like you're untouchable. Your confidence needs to excel at all times, just as if you are ten men. Occasionally, things do go wrong when you humiliate the wrong one or the one who has no sense of humour, leaving you left alone to escape a tricky situation. And, yes, I'd be lying if I said I hadn't had that too. All comics have had their moments, and their narrow escapes or have found themselves in situations that went badly wrong.

I became the heckler who got labelled a dickhead.

I once tried to help a fellow comedian who appeared to be struggling, only to be classed as a dickhead. I found myself turfed out on my ear, ha ha! Totally funny story.

I was at Granada TV watching a program being made, and Ted Robbins was the warm-up comic. I would say he was dying a little, but I suppose as I didn't know him or him me, I didn't really know his act. His act could well have been that way night after night, but anyhow I decided to give him a lift with a few, gentle heckles. The audience roared at me not him, and as I misappropriated his act it seemed I was becoming the better man. So, at the interval, I turned to be confronted by two burly security guards who informed me my night had come to end early. Looking at the size of the two guys, there was definitely no arguing from me. With a wry smile I accepted my punishment and blamed it on the free booze on offer.

I had become a dickhead when I was only trying to help.

So, to finish this section on hecklers and dickheads, I would like to say a little thanks to five fellow comics. Without knowing it, they gave me the material to start my journey as a comedian. Their blue material piss-takes and heckles enabled me to become a fairly decent comic in just a few short years.

Three of those comics, Jimmy Carol, Bernard Manning and Chubby Brown, were all masters of their crafts, but there were two guys in particular that I didn't realise until 2016 were basically the creators of their crafts. One who is no longer with us was Manchester's very own Jackie Carlton. The other was the now Australia-based Al Showman.

They were both masters at taking the piss, and because both were ageing comics and off the scene before I took hold, it meant that I didn't get to realise the other three were almost doing what they'd done years before. I suppose that's like a comic of today hearing me and not realising about the three before me or the two before them, and as I've mentioned only those five, there's still lots of others that even I don't know about and others I do. But, as much as I would like to, I cannot mention them all.

As I leave this section behind with my 12 favourite heckle putdowns, there's one that I've been saying all the years. I can tell you now, it has never failed.

"Ladies and gentlemen, I'd like you all to give that young lad over there a great big round of applause. He's celebrating his very first blowjob, so all his mates have clubbed together and bought him a treble whiskey just so he can get the taste out of his mouth."

Aaaaaaarrrrrggggghhhhh.

My favourite top 12 heckling put downs picked up from years of being on the road

a) See what happens when cousins marry.

b) Good job you're not a prison officer. You don't let any fucker finish a sentence.

c) Hope your next shit's a hedgehog, you twat.

d) Are those your first teeth? They'll be your fuckin last if you speak to me like that again.

e) Go and take your face for a shit.

f) I hope those drugs don't wear off.

g) Do you play bingo? Because your fuckin number's coming up in a minute.

h) Hope you win the raffle. It's an iron, you scruffy bastard.

i) Have you ever had your head between a woman's legs? Because that's what you'll be getting. A fuckin crack in the mouth.

j) Sorry, I don't do requests.

k) You're alright, pal, I was like you after my first pint.

l) Excuse me, can someone call the drug squad? There's 150lb of dope sat over there.

5
COMEDY HEROES

Every comic or comedian has, at some point, sought a form of inspiration from their own comedic heroes. I would say, however, their favoured mentors do change, be it through age or the fact that their own experience allows the pupils to outgrow the masters.

When I was younger, or should I say long before I even had thoughts about being a stand-up comedian, I would settle for being the class clown as I got inspiration from the likes of Norman Wisdom, Jerry Lewis, Abbot and Costello, Benny Hill, Leslie Philips, Sid James, Freddie Starr and my number one top of the list, the fantastic comedy actor Mr Terry Thomas. Terry's portrayal of a nice and friendly tax avoider in the film *Too Many Crooks*, prompted me and my son to have our photographs taken as the character Terry played in the film.

The wonderful Terry Thomas.

Me doing Terry Thomas from *Too Many Crooks*.

My son. Allan, doing Terry as well. Ha ha.

I was also a fond admirer of the 60s and 70s comedy characters in many of the black and white and Ealing comedies, especially the characters that made up the cast of the *Carry On* films. Both male and female, all were worthy of my admiration.

As I sit and write this very day, slapstick comedy is what really aches my ribs. One film that supplied it in droves was *Home Alone* (especially the scene where young Macaulay Culkin fights off the two bandits with trickery and traps). Another film is *Rat Race*, which had me rolling around the cinema in fits of laughter at the sketches where things went pear-shaped. Me and my son laughed so loud that other cinema-goers who weren't as amused as us seemed to laugh more at our laughing.

I recently watched a couple of films done by Sacha Baron Cohen. There were parts of those films where, if I didn't stop myself from laughing so much, I feel I would have curled up and died. It wasn't just my ribs that were killing. I thought my heart was going to leap straight from my chest.

Another of my comedy favourites was Freddie Starr. He had the ability to make people laugh just by his presence.

I did later learn that it only comes when the artiste is well known and is able to ooze with confidence. An unknown comic would, without a doubt, struggle to achieve the same.

When I was learning my apprenticeship (so to speak), I watched, learnt and stole material from the circuit. As a test to the memory of anyone who frequented the cabaret scene throughout the 70s, 80s and 90s, here's a quick list of some of the top comedy show groups and almost every comedian and comedy show group that graced the circuit. The list is endless, but I feel that each and every person reading this list will, at some point, have seen a live show from at least one or more of the artistes listed.

The Grumbleweeds, The Barron Knights, Candlewick Green, Black Onyx, Schooner Fiddlygig, The New Vaudeville Band, The Black Abbots, Freddy Phillips and Beano, The Cresters, The Ivy League, The Druids, The Fortunes, The Chimes, Tomfoolery Highway, The Gary de Paul Showband, Spottymolldoon, The Nobodies, The Black Abbots, Johnny Harper and Headcase, The Royal Variety Showband, Albert Dock, Smiffy, The Mimics, and, last but no means least, The Don Juans.

With comedians, you had a list of comedians that were household names, and then an even longer one of comics who just never quite made the grade. It wasn't because they weren't good enough, but because they just never got the break. They may well have made a living, but, in my eyes, they too missed the boat. Here's a sample of comics who both made it and some that didn't.

Roy Chubby Brown, Bernard Manning, Ken Dodd, Stan Boardman, Mike Lancaster, Dudley Doolittle, Jim Davidson, Austin F Knight, Jimmy Carol, Jimmy Jones, Scully, Max Pressure, Albi Senior, Frankie Allen, Gary Skyner, Buzzer Jones, Jackie Carlton, Jerry Harris, Bunny Lewis, Foo Foo Lamarr, Ricky Livid, Johnny Harper, Cannon and Ball, Little and Large, Dustin Gee, Johnny Goon Tweed, Mike Cash, Crissy Rock, Kelly Fox, Bobby Bender, Al Showman, Trevor Wallace, Jimmy Cricket, John Robinson Junior, Dave Barron, Billy Pearce, Roy Jay, Johnny Casson, Bobby Thompson, Venn Tracy, Pauline Daniels, Dolly Dee, Tom Pepper, Ken Goodwin, Colin Crompton, Bob Monkhouse, Billy Connolly, Peter Kay, Eddie Izzard, Lee Evans, Jack Dee, Seymour Mace, Ricky Livid, Paul Tonkinson, and Frank Skinner.

The list could well go on and on.

Sincere apologies to those whose names don't appear on my list. I know there's a pile more, but I can't name everyone. To all those involved in such acts, a great big thank you for the hours and hours of laughter you gave, not just to me but the whole baying comedy public.

As I left the comedy showbands behind (as did many a front man to become a sole stand up), I still sought to source my material and jokes from comics in all walks of life.

For every comic that was a household name, there were at least 200 that weren't. You just had to have lady luck on your side, and, in some cases, it wasn't what you knew, but who.

To make it to the very top is difficult. It's a long and winding very tough road. There were several absolutely fantastically funny and polished comics that just never quite got that big break. It does grate a little and, although it paid well on some occasions, it is a little annoying when you see the level that some reach and you can't quite seem to get there, knowing full well that on that big stage you could more than hold your own.

As we hit the 90s, the emergence of so-called alternative comedy put most of the clubland comics in the shade, not because they were funnier, but because times change and the direction of comedy was following America. It was all about observational comedy and stories. The days of jokes about the mother-in-law and the wife were going. We had comedians like Lee Evans, Jack Dee, Eddie Izzard, Frank Skinner, Peter Kay and John Bishop.

So, heroes have come and heroes have gone, but the man who remains at the top for me throughout all the years is Terry Thomas. Especially with his portrayal of a tax avoider in *Too Many Crooks*, a film from the 1960s. Some fan I am, though, because, as long as I've known him, I only discovered in 2016 that Terry Thomas told jokes. I found him telling a joke about a budgerigar. It's on YouTube, and, boy is it funny. Believe it or not, the joke is well over 45 years old, and is still brilliant.

Terry Thomas. If anyone sees him, tell him this gag, and show him this book. The gag is on YouTube with the title *Terry Thomas Tells a Joke (Rare)*.

So, here's the Terry Thomas gag, word for word.

It's a joke about a man who lost his wife, rather carelessly, and he was saying how very sorry he was about this to a friend of his at work.

The friend said, "Well, you miss her, do you?"

"Yes, I miss her. I miss the talk in the evening."

So, he said, "Well, buy a budgie".

He said "A what?"

"A budgerigar. You know, a little bird", he said. "Buy it cos they talk. Very nice and you'll cheer you up no end".

So he saw him a couple of days later.

He said, "Did you get the budgie?"

He said, "I did actually".

"Does it talk?" he said.

"No, it doesn't talk at all."

"Dun he?" he said. "Mmmm, that's unusual", he said. "I tell you what. Buy him a mirror. He will have a look a himelf in the mirror. Probably start talking to himself. Try it," he said.

"I will."

Saw him again few days later.

He said, "You get the mirror?"

He said, "Yes, I got the mirror".

"Is he talking?"

"No, not a word", he said. "I tell you what to do. Buy him a bell. That'll do the trick. A bell. He'll sort of nibble about with his beak and he'll talk alright. Buy him a bell."

Saw him a couple of days later.

"You get the bell?

"Yes, I got the bell."

"Is he talking?"

"No, not talking," he said.

"I'll tell you what to do. Buy him a little ladder. Maybe he's a bit liverish. That's why he's not talking. Get the ladder. He'll run up and down and he'll talk."

Saw him a couple of days later. It was three days actually. It was a long weekend, I remember.

I said, "Is he talking?"

"No," he said, "He's dead".

"He's dead?"

"Yes. He's dead."

"Corrr."

"He did say something just before he died," he said.

"What was it?"

"He said... food."

6
THE NEXT GREAT GAG

ALL COMEDIANS LITTER THEIR ACTS WITH GAGS, stories, routines, one-liners, micky-takes, songs and parodies. Inside all that lot there's always a great gag. It's the one they love telling, the one gag that never fails to hit the spot that has an audience in stitches, and basically can be a life saver.

Me personally, I would class such gags as the golden nugget. It's not very often you have two or three of them gems of a gag in your locker at the same time. My golden gag was there for me to get the audience in the palm of my hand, and I would often try and save it for as long as possible before I'd unleash it on my audience. In some instances, that great gag has been a life saver.

As comedians, we're often told gags by the members of an audience they'd just entertained, me included. Well, if I'm honest, if I had one pound for every person that came up to me and said, "Have you heard this one?" I'd be a rich man by now (ha ha).

During the years I was doing stand-up, I told hundreds of gags but only a handful were ever classed as the great gag. From the collection over the years, here are some of the ones I told. Of all the gags I told, my favourite all-time joke, I thought was good from the very start right up until we reached the punchline, I thought the punchline was the weakest part of the gag, and I tried for years to find a better ending. I first heard the gag told by Roy Chubby Brown, but research tells me that gag was around a lot longer than when he started telling it. Chubby's version was by far the funniest of all the versions I heard and the gag (let me tell you) is the 'Bear Hunting' joke. It's related in a couple of pages.

My List of Favourite All-Time Great Gags

1. The gates… the gates have gone.
2. The bin bag the arse has fell out of.
3. The kid with the train set.
4. The cross-country jogger.
5. Have a look in her mouth.
6. Put the sandwiches up myself.
7. Keep till after the wedding.
8. The emerald brooch.
9. Charity do for Prince Charles.
10. The budgerigar.
11. Young lad gets first blow job.
12. The bear hunting trip.
13. The dog that's hard as nails.
14. You can keep the fuckin egg.
15. The taxman. Well, you started it!
16. I'm under the stairs.
17. Mustard, custard and you, you big shit.
18. That's my mother, you shagged mine.
19. Don't know what that chicken said!
20. Venereal disease. Oh, gee, I'm a gonorrhea.

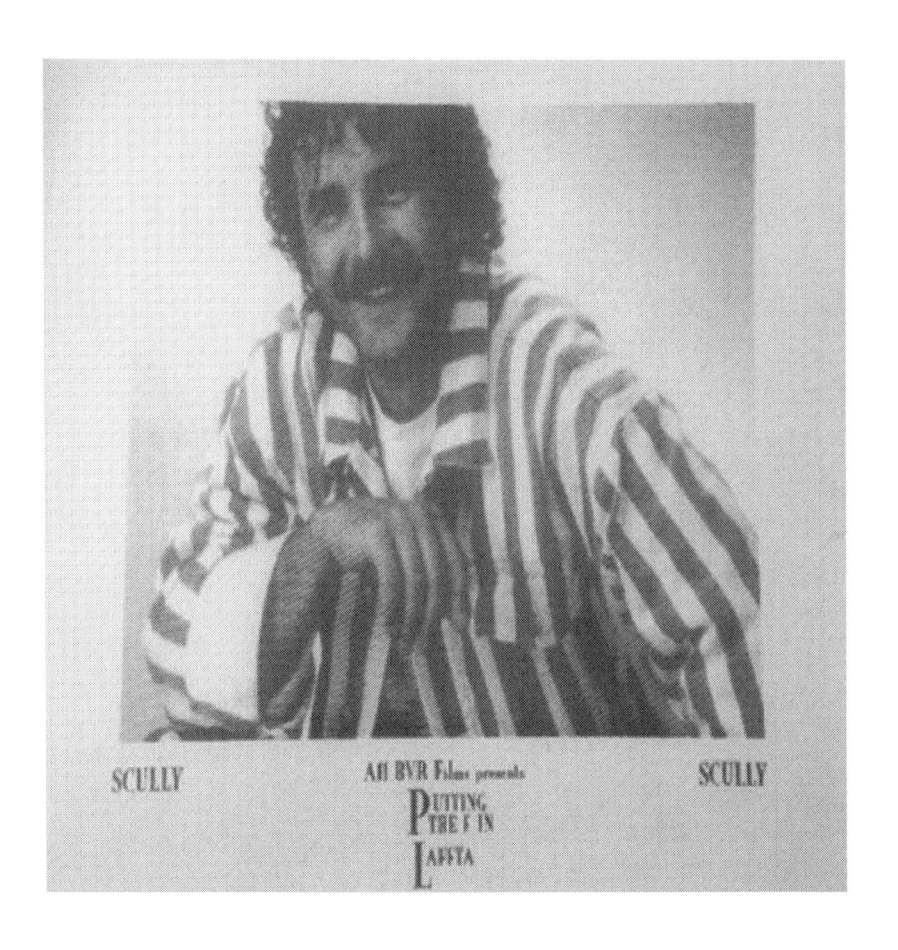

SCULLY An BVR Films presents SCULLY
Putting
The F in
Laffta

Because of the number of great gags, it would be impossible to relate them all, so here are a few I've handpicked.

THE BLACK BIN BAG

Two guys yapping away. One said "I'm sick of the wife. She does my head in". The other guy said, "Kill her. Kill the bitch". "I can't do that," he said, "how would I get rid of the body?" The guy said, "When do your bin men come?" "Monday morning." "Right then. Sunday, kill her, chop her up in bits and put her in black bin bags. Monday morning, leave her out for the bin men. They will take her. Job sorted.

So, Sunday night just as she's nagging again, he stabs her 158 times (he couldn't turn off the bread knife). Then he chops her up and puts her in six bin bags. Monday morning arrives, he puts the bags out, and then he's peeping through the curtains as the bin men arrive and take away the bags. He's rubbing his hands and smiling as there's a knock at the door. It's a bin man. He shits himself as he opens the door. The bin man says, "Have you any more bin bags, sir? The arse has fallen out of this one!"

THE SANDWICHES

Lunch time on the building site, and all the workers head to the canteen. In the brew cabin, a joiner opens up his sandwiches. "Oh bollocks, not corned beef again. I'm sick of corned beef." He's fuming. Just then, the plumber walks in, opens up his sandwiches and shouts "Fuckin beetroot, I'm sick of beetroot. My tongue's red. My arse is red. I'm pissing red." He was furious. Just then, in walks Paddy. He picks his sandwiches up and launches them straight in the bin. "Fuckin cheese," he shouts, "I'm sick of fuckin cheese". The joiner and plumber look on, amazed. "How did you know they were cheese, Paddy?" asked the joiner. "You never even opened them up!" Paddy said, "I know they are cheese. I put the Fokkers up myself".

THE BEAR HUNTING JOKE

(So, I first came across this joke as told by Roy Chubby Brown, but, when I researched it, I found just like everything else in comedy there's nothing new. Jokes just get told a different way by different comedians. I heard several versions of this joke, but most had the same ending. That was a shame because the punch-line (the ending) is the weakest part of the gag. I've tried to come up with a different ending but still nothing I found was strong enough and I will say that the version I liked most was Chubby Brown's. He is still the master.)

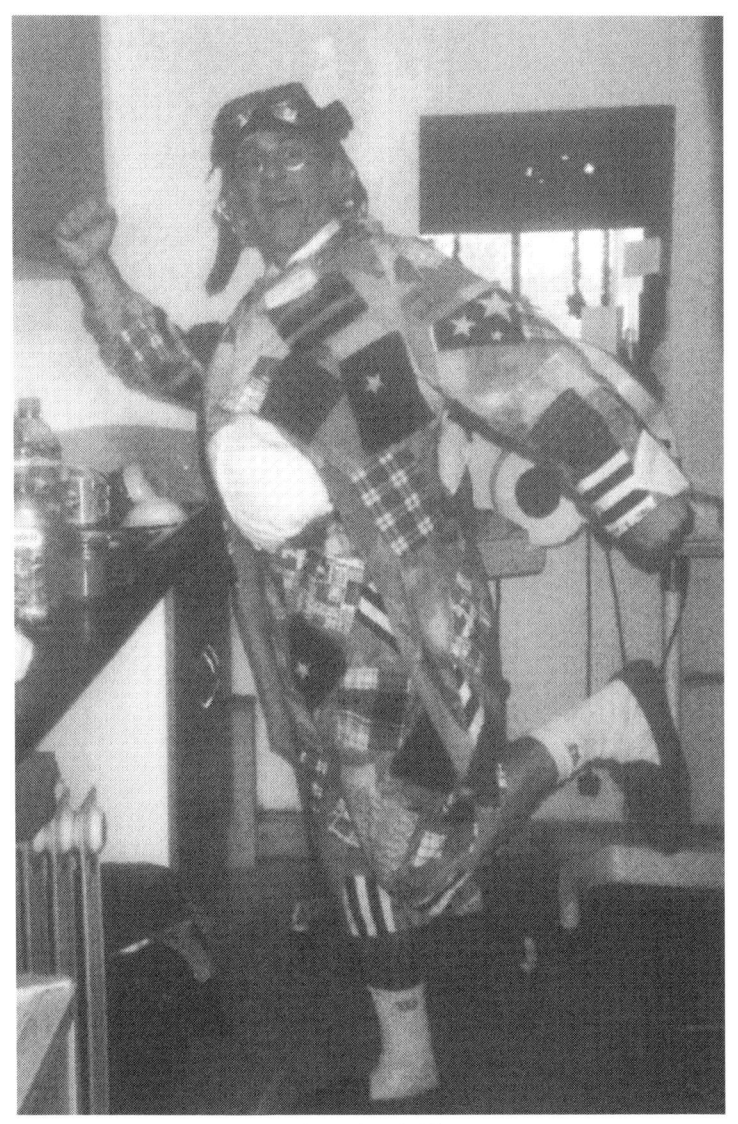

Me, dressed as Chubby Brown.

'M NOT SAYING WE'VE ALL GOT ONE, BUT MOST OF US know of one. I'm talking of a best mate that we all envy. You know the type. A right good looking bastard. Ha ha. Look at your faces. I can picture most of you smiling, thinking "He's talking about me". Well, I'm talking the type of guy born with a silver spoon in his gob. The type that when he bends over, the sun's rays that shine from his arse would light up a room and melt an ice lolly in seconds. You know the type I'm talking about. Perfect head of hair, all his own teeth, not a single filling in any tooth, eyes that could read a number plate from a different continent, a perfect tan you'd pay a fortune for from a bottle or a sunbed... And the best bit... he's got a string of gorgeous girls queuing up to suck him off without him having to return the favour. He drives all the best cars. BMWs, Jags, Mercedes... doesn't even know what a fuckin MOT is.

Then there's the clothes. Immaculately dressed. Gucci, Armani... You name it, he wears it. Thinks Primark is a swear word. Then you look down and he wears shoes you can eat your dinner off.

Even at school, he had it all. Passed all his exams without having to do any revision, always first picked for all the sports teams, loads of money for the tuck shop, never got detention, didn't even know a free dinner ticket existed, got ten GCSEs, eight fuckin O-levels, went to college and university just for the parties, got a degree and walked straight into a well-paid job!

WHAT A CUNT! Me, jealous? Jealous? Me? Am I fu... ckin too right I am. Even now, as adults, he has it all.

It just never ends. Holidays. There's nowhere the fucker hasn't been, nothing the raghead hasn't done. In fact, the only place he hasn't been is the bastard moon. He doesn't even know the jam butty camp at Rhyl exists. He's been to Australia, Brazil, North and South America, Hawaii... He's snorkelled, parachuted, hang glided, skied down the fuckin Swiss Alps, flew on Concorde, the Airbus A380 double bastard decker, the 747 jumbo jet helicopters, hovercrafts, cruised the med on the QE2... You get what I'm saying.

So, picture this. I'm walking through the Trafford Centre and he's there strutting his stuff with his Ray-Bans on. It wasn't even sunny.

"Hiya, mate." (Two-faced fucker, aren't I? Ha ha.) "So, where is it this year then? Tenerife? Bardy fuckin bados?"

"Oh, no," he said. "I'm going bear hunting in Canada."

I said, "Bear hunting in Canada? The bear will rip ya big daft stupid head off. Mess all your fuckin hair up!"

He said "Oh. No, it's all organised. Five star hotel, all-inclusive for a week. A grand! They give you all the gear, snow shoes, hat, rifle , catch-a-bear book... Come back with some prizes".

Well, fuck me. Picture this. Saw him a month later, bandaged to fuck, hair ripped out in clumps, teeth missing... and he was limping.

I thought all my lottery numbers had come in. My smile was that wide I couldn't hide it if I was in a blacked out cave 200 miles under the earth's crust.

"What happened then?"

Dead concerned, sarcastically almost pissing my pants as I was giggling to fuck.

"Well, I was in the forest, I drops me wallet and shit myself."

"What? Was there was a picture of the wife staring up at you?"

He ignores that one, ha ha.

"When I looked up, I spots a bear. Fuckin hell, it was bigger than Paddington. So, I loads the gun, took aim and fuckin fired. Jesus, I thought, I've killed a fuckin bear. I thought, how am I going to carry that home, so I runs over, fucks the bear. It was like shit off a shovel. Just as I'm looking left and right, there's a tap on my shoulder. I turned round. Fuck me! It was like King Kong the bear was stood behind me.

He said. "Have you just fired that gun at me?"

"No."

"Yes. You have singed my fuckin ear. You just shot at me."

"OK, so I have. It's not my fault. You're a big daft bear living in a forest. I'm here from Manchester on a week's holiday. The hotel's nice, lovely food and barrels of free ale. There's a jacuzzi, sauna and swimming pool, and excellent room service."

The bear said, "I'm not fuckin bothered. You just shot at me!"

"OK, so what if I did?."

The bear said, "Fair enough. Drop your fuckin baggy ones."

"Excuse me?"

"You heard, or are you deaf as well as daft?"

"For what?"

"Errr, you do know us bears are almost human as well you know?"

I said, "What?"

He said "Kecks down. Bears like a fumble in the jungle too, you know."

"But, you do know I'm not a bear."

"That's right. Not much chance of us being related then eh?"

The bear grabs his hair to hold on to. Shag shag shag shag, oohhh me fuckin ring piece, and watch me rug twatty bastard.

He limps back into the hotel straight on the bidet. Ooooooh.

Next morning, he's up. Fresh as a daisy. Has a full English with extra beans. Then he's in the hotel shop, buys a bazooka and hand grenades, poisonous tracker snake, ssssssss, a big knife, and a jar of Vaseline.

An hour later, he creeps back into the forest, spots a sign. It says "Bear Left". Then he sees it. The snake goes "ssssssss". I know I know. Knew it was the same bear. Big bandage on its ear. He points the bazooka "puuuuurffff". Fuckin ell, half the forest has gone. Chucks a hand grenade "pkkdgddhjjj", then another just to be on the safe side. Runs over with his big knife.

"I warned you, ya big hairy mother fucka, Fucks, he gone."

He looks at the snake. The snake goes "left right ssssssss left right ssssssss".

Just then, there's a tap on the shoulder. He turns round. Same fuckin bear.

The bear said, "Oh. Not you again".

"Nor, nor, mate, not me again. I'm just down from Glasgow for the weekend. Bit of fishing and shit."

"No, it's you. Fingymagigg from Manchester. You were here yesterday. Shot me fuckin ear off."

"OK, so it was me. I told you yesterday I was here for a week. You knew I'd be back. Didn't you have the sense ta fuckin hibernate. Good thinking, Batman!"

"Fair enough," said the bear. "Drop em!"

"What?"

"Drop the fuckin Pacino's. Not often us grizzlies get to bang a bum two days on the trot."

"What the fuck's up with you? How do bears even know about sex?"

"Course we do. You don't think I've got paws like this through climbing trees do you? We bash our fuckin bishop, like you fuckers."

Shagg shagg shagg shagg, ooooooo me fuckin arse, bastard, twat, cunt, fuckaa.

Next morning he's up before the dawn chorus, the snake goes "ssssssss".

He goes back to the shop and with the last of his travellers' cheques, he buys a tank, and gets to the forest just as the mist is clearing .

The snake's up. "Sssssss," he said.

"You're no fuckin good!"

Stamps on it, highers the tank and fires. Fuckin el, Winnipeg disappears.

He thought, "That's vapourised the big hairy bastard."

He climbs out the tank, runs over to the spot, then tappppp, tappp screws his face up in a gurning.

The bear says, "Let's be honest. You're not just here for the hunting, are you, darling…?"

Got to say this , a good polished comedian could tell this gag and easily stretch it to get between six and eight minutes which basically turns it into a story.

Now, that's an art in itself , turning a gag into a story (isn't it, Mr Venn Tracy ha ha?)

WELL, YOU SHAGGED MINE!!!

The moment has arrived. My 13th birthday. Coincidently, it's my parents' time to enlighten me on the birds and the bees.

Well, I say 'parents'. What I mean is it's my dad's job!

Who'd have thought, hey, that parents are clueless when it comes to this moment in time? I think they just expect you to learn it at school or pick it up off your mates, or even read it from a book .

Either way, I'm a teenager and my dad (bless him), summons me to the garden. He's as nervous as a vicar when the police arrive.

"Look son, there comes a time…"

"Yeah, dad."

"Well, you know, like, there was Adam and Eve."

"Yeah, dad."

I'm thinking "Fukinell, come on dad, spit the fucker out."

"Well, there's the birds and the bees…"

Just then, he reaches to his pocket, and I thought "Fuck me, he's gonna bring out a johnny. Ah, no, its his wallet. I then thinks, "Fuckinell, he's wrote it down for me". Laughing.

"Here's £20 quid," he said. "Get to town. Market Street. Get a hooker and go learn all about it!"

"About what, dad?"

I wanted to watch him squirm.

"Right. That'll do, ya little bastard. Get to town and don't come back till you've had ya 20 quid's worth."

So off I popped. Straight on the bus heading for Market Street, thinking "Yehhh".

It wara lovely sunny day lots of lovely ladies all in miniskirts, tops wi no bra and massive bazookas, just swinging in the joyous weather.

Just then I heard "Scull!"

I turned round. There was me nanna. 50 bags of shopping. There must a bin a sale on at Primark.

"What you doing here?" she said.

"Well. ya know it's me birthday today, nann. I've finally reached 13 and my dad's give me a big fat £20 note to come to town, get a lady of the night that will teach me all about the birds and the bees."

"No!" she said. "I'm not leaving you alone up town. "Come on," she said, "Come back to mine. I'll cook you some dinner".

Half hour later, I was lapping up my favourite beans on toast, followed by sponge pudding and custard and a big fat glass of dandelion and burdock. Just as I finished the glass I heard me nanna shout, "Scully, come upstairs, I've got a little surprise for ya".

I laughed to myself. I thought, "If I go up there, I've got a bigger one for you". I goes up. She's only lay on the bed with fuck all on. "Come on," she said, "I'm going to teach you the lot". Well fuck me. I banged her left right and centre, she sucked me off, I licked her minge, back-scuttled her, doggy-styled her, then finished her off by diving head first off the wardrobe right into that big hairy crevasse of hers. It were great.

I walked home feeling like ten men and thinking I could shag for England! When I got home, dad was sat there with a pint in one hand and a cigar in the other.

"How did you get on lad?" he said, looking at his smiling proud son. "Great, dad, I was in town and bumped into nanna, and as a birthday treat she took me home, she fed me dinner then she taught me the lot, and I've still got me £20."

"Oh my word!" His face went purple and he was raging like a bull. "Do you mean to tell me you've just shagged my mother?"

"Par for the course, dad. You've shagged mine!"

7
LUCKY LAD

I KNOW YOU WOULDN'T ASSOCIATE AN ARTIST AS BEing in a dangerous job, but I will be the first to consider myself a lucky lad. I'm lucky because, in all the years of performing, I can count on one hand the occasions when I encountered dodginess.

Remember I was a blue comedian who took the mickey and (something to bear in mind), and that people the world over weren't given a sense of humour as a birthright. Everyone is different and as they say, some can take it, while others clearly

IF EASILY OFFENDED PLEASE DO NOT ATTEND
FULL SHOW ENQUIRIES CONTACT HARRY BARNES ON:- 061 799 268

cannot. Many a time when a risqué comic is appearing, there's usually an advert to accompany the show and the ad uses phrases like "If easily offended, please stay away" (this was at the bottom of my posters).

That rule is all well and good when people are buying a ticket with the knowledge of who they are going to see. But, as an unknown comic who is booked to appear as part of a venue's weekly entertainment programme, now that's a different ball game. Most people just go for a night out, and the last thing they expect is to be ridiculed at the expense of a comic's performance in search of laughter. And, yes, I've heard it 100 times – "Well, if they don't like it, they shouldn't come". But I never think like that. I always think to myself that I hope they enjoy the show because, in all fairness, it is never my intention to offend anyone. I'd rather not perform than upset people.

One of my first dodgy issues was in St Helens. I was giving one particular guy loads of stick. He seemed to be soaking it up as all around were in fits of laughter. In all fairness, he wasn't. What he was doing was bottling it all up.

I slightly sensed it and started to drift away from him, but as I left him alone the damage was already done. In his eyes, it was too late. Inside, he was seething. The crowd lapped up all the jokes, and he just bottled it all up. The fact that the crowd were loving it pushed him over the edge I'd left him at. Eventually, he blew his top and lunged towards the stage to rip my head off. A few guys stood in his way and held him back, and with microphone in hand, I was reduced to apologising that it was only a bit of fun. Needless to say, this Jack the Lad character was reduced to being a Barbie doll. My act was cremated on the spot. It was a valuable lesson learnt and a very close shave. Phew!

The next was The Star pub in Bury. I'd ridiculed the doorman for most of the first spot, and unbeknown to me, he had very little of a sense of humour. He walked up to me on the stage, and with one punch launched me straight across it. I could do little but to get back on my feet. I came straight back at him to save face, and took the mickey a little more. That's not an action I would repeat or do later on in my career. He decided to leave, but, once again, my act was kaput.

Having said that, I've known a couple of similar-style comedians that weren't as lucky, to the point they have been properly filled in one such incident leading to a court case. I have had a couple of incidents where I've been covered in beer and a jar of nuts slung at me at The Benchill pub in Wythenshawe though it wasn't me directly who was wounded. It was my equipment. I left the stage after my performance, which wasn't one of the best (but personally it wasn't me. it was them). To put it bluntly, I had a crowd of what we term as heads. Wannabe gangsters. When not on stage, I'd usually have a bit of music playing just to keep the atmosphere going till the night finished. While getting changed, I heard the music stop and, thinking the tape had finished, returned to the stage only to find the group of lads sat at the front had decided to launch all my equipment evenly around the pub. I was peeved, but not mental.

I wasn't about to stand up to them for the sake of a few pieces of equipment. I did a lot of gigs and ridiculed more than a handful, but, all in all, I figure myself as one hell of a lucky lad!

I've recently been on a few dinners (in a 'night out' capacity), and on at one particular dinner was a comic I've known for a lot of years. Bobby Bender was the comic. He's a little older than myself, but has the same style of comedy.

I knew this fact anyway but it made me realise even more so that my choice to quit was the right one, his style of risqué comedy I felt put him in a vulnerable position, danger wise, but for whatever reason it's his own choice to soldier on.

8
WORKING WITH STRIPPERS

Of all the gigs I did – cabaret, mixed, stag shows, hen nights, late night shows, early mornings, and all dayers, the one I disliked the most was working with female strippers. They were sometimes good to look at, but a real chore to work with. I had no choice in the matter as it was all part and parcel of the job.

A Gents Night came with comedian and strippers (or female dancers to put it into a more complimentary context). The male strippers were never really a problem. In fact, it was great working with males because they not only gave value for money, they were surrounded by horny females. Ha ha.

Female strippers were often a nightmare. They were forever thinking they were either actresses or anything other than a plain old stripper, while trying their best to get paid for doing the very minimum.

The best ever line that most of them used in pursuit of getting away with doing as little as possible was, "We only do one long spot".

It's meant to be every man's dream to work with female strippers (all those tits and fannies right there in front of your mince pies and under your nose, and big hairy beavers staring right back at ya). But my experience isn't all it's cracked up to be. Working with the females can be a nightmare, and that fact is fuelled because the majority of the time, the women knew just how to get their own way with the people who had booked us and that was mostly men.

In all the years I've seen them come and go, from the old dears to the new young ones just coming through, I've probably got a lifetime of stories, but I'm pretty sure just a few may have you running to the bathroom.

Just to make the lads jealous, here's Scully and the Playgirls.

I did end up friends with some strippers, but I couldn't wait to see the back of others – almost as quickly as I met them.

I can tell a few stories and I have no need to mention any names. If any of them ever read my story they would probably know its them I'm talking about.

When I first started working with strippers, it was mostly the older and more experienced girls who generally had a half-decent act, not just get on stage, do a little dance, wiz the clothes off and fuck off. There was one called Eve. She always gave value for money. There were Chrissy and Marie, Indian Jacky, Juicy Jane (one of the younger ones), Gillian and Cameo… As you can imagine, these are all their stage names.

I can hear you saying now "I bet you shagged them all". Well, the answer is no!

And, let me say that just because a lady strips her clothes off willy nilly, it doesn't make them easy. It was just their attitude that was a fukka. They were all tossers. Even though there were some pretty good-looking, horny bitches that most men would have given their right arm to get a frollickin in the back room with, I've absolutely no doubt that if all the females were present in one room right now 75 to 80% would not have a good word to say about me either.

When it came to running a show, I feel I was quite organised and regimental and that was something that most of the girls found hard to either deal with or accept. A stripper could turn up half hour late and still want to be bought a drink and given time to dolly-bird themselves up before hitting the stage. They never really felt the pressure the comedian had in tying the show up, making sure all went well and that the crowd got their money worth in terms of entertainment.

Male strippers, on the other hand, were a lot easier to work with. They were fully focused and prepared to give not just their money worth, but go over and above the call of duty.

The rewards for the males weren't just the cash they got at the end but more often than not, they got rewards from the ladies. I mean, let's have it right. Where else can you go on a night out (because that's what hen nights are) and have horny women offering you it on a plate without so much as a chat-up line, or having to buy them a drink or offer them a dance.

My early days of Ladies Nights saw me work with the likes of Adam, Ricky Day and Master Gee, then we had the likes of Master C, Boy Blue, The Enforcer, Sex Machine, Randy Marcus, Andy King and Little Boy Blue aka Lash, Harry Webb, (and bless my old mate) Simon Whipping Boy. RIP, Simon. We lost him in a car crash in the 90s.

Going back to the female strippers, they weren't all the same. They were either clean or blue. The clean girls just did the straightforward stripping, while the blue girls were the ones the bucket went round for. Nudge, nudge, wink, wink.

With the emergence of lap dancing bars, a lot of lap dancers thought they could cross over into stripping.

ALLAN BIRKIN

Not once did I come across a lap dancer that had an act. Most of the strippers with acts would do fire eating and one even smoked a cigar through her honey pot. In the early days of working with the females, I came unstuck by still being around when the girls were performing the whip round session. More often than not, it led to problems. A girl would say she wanted x to perform that spot, so the bucket would go round and while most would be fair in what they chucked in the bucket, others would just give spare copper, leading the girls to say there's not enough to perform, then refusing to participate. That would lead to drunken men wanting to fight the world. I soon learnt that I wasn't getting paid to be part of the shenanigans, so I made my excuses and left before it even got organised.

On a different side, I once felt so sorry for a blue girl on a Sunday afternoon show where she offered to do the whip round spot. The money collected amounted only to about £6 because of the coppers chucked in. She refused to do it, and was threatened with her life so she performed, but she lived to work again, and I'm pretty sure she learnt well from the experience. After spending years working with strippers, this was always one little gripe I had.

When working with the males, it was the fact that with women, if you flash them a little bit of dick, they are like putty in your hands. I used to work my tripe off entertaining, then I would try selling my merchandise. It was like flogging a dead horse. The males would flash their knob and, fuck me, there was a cue as long as my arm for their signed photos that inevitably ended up on the table soaked in beer.

I secretly longed for a piece of their action and in 1996/7 on the back of the success of *The Full Monty* film, I got my chance. A couple of my football friends approached me to help them set up a *Full Monty* troupe to work on the Ladies Nights. Not only did I help them, I joined up. Yessssss, the best three years of my showbiz career! My kit came off and I loved every minute of my time as a male stripper. Get in! Ha ha.

Doing The Full Monty.

As the popularity of T*he Full Monty* began to wane, I realised that my comedic days were on the wane too. It didn't take much to realise I was coming to the end of my showbiz days. The signs were written on the wall. I was enjoying it less and less, especially the travelling, the waiting around the rubbish gigs, and carrying equipment around (and all for what?) I'd travelled the length and breadth of the country performing but I realised sooner rather than later that I was never going to amount to anything more than just a jobbing clubland comic.

THE FULL MONTY

In a mental attempt to up my profile, in the build up to the *Who's an Ugly Bastard?* video release we set up at the Glasgow Pavilion in Scotland for Scully's Strip-r-oke – a late show where normal punters could act out their stripping fantasies on the big stage.

It caused eruptions, both in the press and at the theatre on the night. It was a midnight show so it didn't finish till the early hours. There was no shortage of contestants who were keen to get both their hands on the cash and the chance of a little future career. But its controversy put it in the national press, thus causing it to be kiboshed as quickly as it was started. Strip-r-oke was over.

WE CERTAINLY CREATED PUBLICITY WITH OUR STRIP-R-OKE.

9
REMEMBERING ALL THE JOKES

WHEN YOU'RE THE TYPE OF COMEDIAN THAT I WAS, you'll notice many others who appear to be the *bang bang bang* type with all their jokes, one-liners, mickey-takes, and their ability to deal with hecklers at lightning speed). To the untrained eye it can seem like it's all *off the cuff* and *ad libbed*.

But, trust me, I'm not lying when I say it isn't. I speak for both myself and other comedians when I say it's all a very well-rehearsed and practiced routine.

You often get asked, "How on earth do you remember all those jokes?" Well, believe you me, as well as being a fairly good ad libber, the majority of the act and all the material is very well rehearsed and well performed. When I say 'rehearsed', I don't mean sat in front of a mirror talking to yourself, I mean telling the gag on a stage. That's how we comedians get it right, by telling it night after night. To me, it's just like anybody else doing their job. You get to a point where you're able to do it just like a car engine that's being driven in overdrive.

In the days when I was at the end of my performing life, and realised I didn't want to do it any more, I would search for excuses as to why I couldn't make the forthcoming gig on Thursday or Friday. Yet, for years I had prided myself on never letting anyone down.

Here's a good example of this overdrive philosophy. I was about to go on stage in Yorkshire and was sitting in the dressing room all changed and ready to go on. But all that was going through my mind was "I don't want to be here". I just wanted to get in my car and go home, but then I heard the compere utter the immortal words:

"LADIES AND GENTLEMEN, PLEASE PUT YOUR HANDS TOGETHER AND WELCOME ON STAGE THE ONE AND ONLY…"

I was announced onto the stage and bounced on, picked up the microphone and as I started the first song, the thought was still going through my head. "I don't want to be here". And, what do you know, as if by magic, my performance came to an end. That show was just performed on overdrive.

I'd just completed 45 minutes and brought the house down. For any person who has a lot on their mind (and I always have all sorts going through my head), the one and only time my mind is ever clear with no thoughts whatsoever, is the moment I walk off a stage. Purely because for 45 minutes I'd only been thinking about the jokes I was telling, and nothing else. And, two minutes after my performance came to an end, I was back to square one and all thoughts of everything else returned.

So, as for remembering the jokes and scripts, they are all well-rehearsed. Having a large repertoire of jokes and stories enables you to perform longer – as long as you can remember it all of course.

MISSED THE BOAT

PUTTING IT ALL TOGETHER
The infamous cards of routines with five or six one-liners.

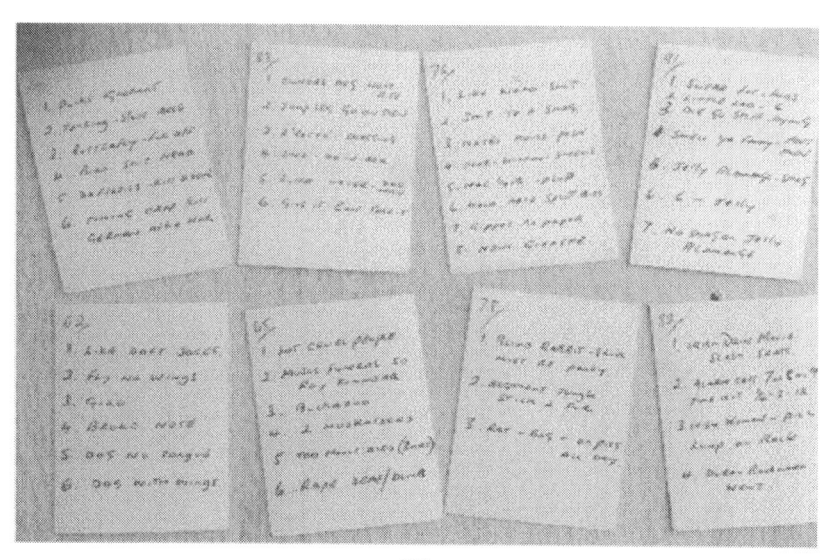

I did try to study how Chubby Brown was able to churn out material, second after second, minute after minute and come up with a fairly new act every time I went back to see him.

Without having it confirmed by the man himself, I came up with my own conclusion, and this is my interpretation of how it was possible.

I realised it was a simple process. You would learn your jokes and lines in a set of maybe four, five or six. Your first six would be classed as your routine number one, your second six would then become your number two, and so on and so forth. So, if you were asked to recite the sixth line in routine number 12 or 22, you could.

So, basically, your act would made up of about 50 groups of six gags or lines, intertwined with you going off in different tangents and then returning back to the point where you got distracted. Then, any new sets of six (perhaps numbers 51 52 53 etc) would then become the new beginning to your act.

So, if you did a gig on the 1st of January and started with the first 50 numbers… 1) Six jokes then 2) Six jokes and so on up to the final six gags of your act which would be routine number 50.

OMG, I can hear some other comics saying "What the fuck's he on about? This guy's a dick" Ha ha.

I can understand that, though. I'm not speaking for all comedians, because we're not all the same. This, may I add, is my tried and tested approach.

Back to the story. So, the next six lines with all your new jokes would then be put at the beginning of your act meaning your gig on the 1st of March would be started with numbers 51) Six jokes into 52) Six jokes into 53) Six jokes at which point you'd hit number 1 again. So, you'd do 1) Six jokes up to 47, leaving out 48 49 and 50, or doing them as well and performing longer thus making your beginning look like you have a different act.

It sounds a little confusing, but when you are as hard a working comic such as the likes of Chubby Brown, with new material coming in all the time, that's how his act changes so often. Other comics such as big Bernard Manning basically used the same act for years and years. I know he would say, "If it isn't broke, don't fix it", but with the likes of Chubby (who plays to sell-out crowds repeatedly paying good money) you have to put the work in, and that means graft.

Nowadays, when I do the odd performance, because I'm not on the ball, my timing, delivery and memory are all over the place. I need to place reminders on the floor in front of me to help me remember all my jokes and routines. It only takes possibly one word to jig the memory of a whole host of gags, although in my older age I often hear the words from some smart arse in the crowd – *"You've just told that one!"*

Another killer of old age is when you start to tell a gag on overdrive but realise half way through that you can't remember the second bit, nor the punchline.

Now, that is funny!

10
CAN I TELL YOU THIS ONE?

"Eee are mate I've got one for ya!"
"No!"

BEING A STAND-UP COMIC, I CAN'T SAY I'VE HEARD every joke, but I've certainly heard a few. A real pet hate is when one of the punters comes up with that most famous of lines "I've got one for you", or "Have you heard this one?" Nine times out of ten I've heard it, but don't want to seem rude, so have no choice but to go along with them and listen. I try my best to let them believe I haven't heard that one.

I've come to realise there's nothing better than a punter thinking they've provided you with a little part of your future act. Cue the fake laugh at the punchline that I already knew was coming. It's not nice to ruin their big moment. Occasionally, a punter will come up with a gem and a cracker of a gag, and that's worth buying them a drink for.

Three of my friends, and believe it or not, the happy bunny on the left knew a joke or two!

I hope it doesn't make me sound ungrateful or rude because I'm eternally grateful for my audiences, their input, the odd gag, and their criticism as it all contributed to my act.

ON THE SUBJECT OF "CAN I TELL YOU THIS ONE?"

THIS ONE'S NOWT TO DO WITH THE JOKES, FOLKS.

Of all my years in this business, I've met some very nice people. One guy I'd like to mention and bring to your attention is Mr Henry Harrison, the original drummer from The New Vaudeville Band (hit singles *Winchester Cathedral* and *Finchley Central).*

I first met Henry in the 1980s when I saw The New Vaudeville Band, performing at The Willows in Salford. Henry also ran an agency called NVB Entertainments. We worked for him several times over the years and me and Henners have stayed friends to this day. I love Henry to bits, alongside his wife Fran and all their children. My claim to fame is that I once depped on the drums for Henry, doing a week with The New Vaudeville Band. I loved playing to Dr Jazz.

Henry's great claim to fame is he once saw ELVIS PRESLEY LIVE IN CONCERT.

All the best, Henry, keep up the swearing."I faking lave him!!"

NOW, CAN I SHOW YOU THIS ONE?
"Henry"

My mate, Henry Harrison

11
PLACES TO WORK

AS AN ACCOMPLISHED PERFORMER, I CAN TELL YOU that I've worked in virtually all counties of the country, and believe you me, they are all different. Over the years, I had favourite places to work, and also came across places I vowed I'd never return to!

In the early days, I used to thrive on working the toughest areas like Liverpool and the north east. Liverpool was a hard one because they were all comics and forever tried to get the better of you. When I was young, I loved that challenge, but as I got older I became tired of the struggle to bash the comic. So much so that, in the end, I refused offers of gigs in that area.

One of the most difficult areas to work was the north east. As a Sunday lunchtime comic, they'd just stare you out as you hit them with both barrels, then, all of a sudden, you'd come out with a gem, and they would be crying laughing. The ice was broken, and you would enjoy and relish the rest of the show. Working the north east made you tough. You had to work for your supper, and that had a bonus side because, when you returned to work in a different area the next day, your confidence allowed you to storm the gig with ease.

There were plenty of areas that were appreciative just to have entertainment on and not only lapped it up but relished in it. These were areas that were tucked out of the way, like inner Wales and the countryside. Major holiday resorts are more difficult to work as they've seen every comic, heard every singer, danced to every band and watched (back to front) every trick a magician has up his sleeve.

I didn't relish working the south either. For some strange reason, cockneys just don't warm to us northerners. They are a bit like southern drivers. If you want to be let out at a junction when driving your car, I'm afraid your odds are better for a lottery win than getting a 'waving you out' hand. We northerners can't warm to the majority of cockneys either, although we are far more easy-going than our counterparts.

One place I never managed to work was Ireland, even though I was told on many occasion "They'd love you over there". Looking at the success of Brendan Carroll – a comedian I classed as older but with similar styles to myself – the commentors were probably right!

I did do three spells in Benidorm for a week at a time, but the last time I did it, I vowed it would be the last. I was on with good old Eric Delaney the fantastic drummer (RIP). Right up to the day he died, he put on a fantastic show and his stamina was incredible. The problem with working in Benidorm was that my first spot was at 11pm and the second was at 3am. This was a nightmare to work because all the holiday makers were leathered, and I was just a 'bang bang bang' merchant. It was awful to work.

I did do many a year at The Jaggy Thistle in Blackpool which was a stomping ground for many of the Scots who invaded Blackpool for many of the summer weekends.

On another note, over the years I always took a video camera with me, so have lots of my performances on record (thanks, Duane, my camera man). They remain as proof and testament to both myself and others that I performed at a high level of entertainer.

When it comes to the places to work, just as there were preferred areas, and there were also favourite venues to work. It was great to work at a venue where everything was set up correctly – the stage, lights, sound, and (most importantly) the punters.

Venues such as The Willows in Salford and The Talk of the North in Eccles, were just two of the bigger venues. There were several pub venues that. in true form. tried to imitate the nightclubs by providing all those good bits. The Lightbowne Hotel in

Moston (which was owned by the late Foo Foo Lamarr), gave you all the assets of a top cabaret venue with compere, great musicians on organ and drums, good stage, sound and lights, a top of the bill slot, and of course and most importantly, a good and appreciative audience. Top venue all round.

A sample of tickets for my gigs.

It's a funny thing. You've spent the majority of your life working on the circuit and have worked hundreds of venues in hundreds of areas. Although the large majority of the venues you performed in have long since gone, you can't but help some things. Like when you're driving around, saying either to your passenger or even yourself if you're alone, "I worked there",

"I've done that place", "I remember doing that one", "Died on my arse there", "Stormed that gaff, "Got paid off there", "That crowd were shite etc". Ha ha, done that, been there wore the t-shirt, and starred in the video as well!

The many areas I worked, at the height of their popularity, usually had a guide or booklet that included all the venues and the artistes that were booked to appear. I did keep a massive collection and have included a picture of just a few that lie beneath a blanket of dust from all these years on my shelves. They are probably worth a small fortune as collectors' pieces to sentimental artistes.

Around Yorkshire, we had the fantastic *Clubman's Guide*. For every venue and every act, it was like a bible, and if you made the front cover… well, you felt you'd kind of made it!

12
TAKING A BREAK

THEY DO SAY TO BE CAREFUL WHAT YOU WISH FOR.

I'd been onstage almost every week, and nightly since I was 17 or 18, and I longed for a break.

Because I was now pro and it was my living, it wasn't that easy. Well, I suppose it was, but I just didn't get around to it.

I felt like I just needed a twelve-month break.

A whole year without picking up a microphone and gracing a stage.

In the latter years I was only grossing about £12,000 a year so I worked out that with no petrol expenses or agents commission, I just needed about £9,000 or £10,000 to take that break.

The answer was almost upon me in 2002. I sold my house and that was just what the doctor ordered. I could have my year out.

Now when they say to be careful what you wish for, it's exactly what it means. That year out spread to two, then three, and, before I knew it, there was no going back.

In the years of doing the circuit, one night I was here and the next I was there.

It seemed glamorous, but as much as I enjoyed life on the road, glamorous it wasn't. It was a lonely existence.

When all your friends are settling down after tea to watch *Emmerdale* and *Corrie*, you're tear-arsing up the M62 to make them laugh.

It did, however, give me the opportunity to see a lot more of the country, well more than most, and it gave me a far better opportunity to meet people than I would have in an ordinary nine to five job.

There's still the very odd gig here and there that I get asked to do, but, as for being a pro again, that's definitely a no-no. Unless, for some reason, I end up skint and have no choice but to fight for my supper.

I also had in my mind that I didn't want to be one of those very few entertainers that didn't quite know when to quit. I didn't want to die on the stage, so I quit.

On that note, I will say that a few friends are still working the circuit, and (I have to be honest) feel they are too old to still be doing it. But, it's their choice, no matter how ridiculous it looks, no names mentioned (Gay Boy, Billy Butler, and I was going to say Sweens, but he will kick my head in).

13
MY ADVICE

(Jack of all trades... Master of none)

'VE OFTEN FELT I'M GOOD AT OFFERING ADVICE (though I'm never good at taking it ha ha), especially when you can teach someone in minutes what has taken you and others years to learn. But that's just me. Others are not so forthcoming in allowing you the shortcuts, especially if it is their livelihood that's in threat of being challenged.

It's a bit like rubber-necking in road traffic. I would always go down a different lane and squeeze in. But, just as I would do it, I would also let somebody else in if they chose to go down the same path. As the saying goes, this world is big enough for the both of us. I don't take kindly to do-gooders and busybodies who try their utmost to prevent you doing just this.

On a different subject, I was once playing the drums on a jam night in Middleton. I was drumming along to *Long Train Running*. With my years of experience, I used to play a rhythm to that song that I was unable to explain in depth, although I could play it. I was then asked by a young enthusiastic drummer eager to learn what that rhythm was I was belting out. I was slightly embarrassed and did my utmost to explain it to him that years of playing had enabled me to do it, but I couldn't explain to him how! I must have sounded arrogant to the young lad. If so, I apologise and stress that I wasn't. Sorry, mate. I've often been somewhere on a night out where I wasn't working, but I was like everybody else and just an audience member. I always try to offer advice, especially when I'm watching learning artistes trying their best in all aspects to perform, as well as seeking out the minor details like the sound, stage setting and format. But I don't tell them I'm a fellow performer and come across as someone who should just sit down and mind his own business ha ha.

I would also like to mention a couple of injustices and point out that the karma thing is not just a myth, and neither is "What goes around, comes around". In the event where you don't get justice, you just have to bite the pillow and just let society stick one right up your arse.

I once got a speeding ticket created by the old-fashioned method of a copper pointing a so-called laser at you from a different country, and their word was law! I was no more speeding than Percy the snail, or Tommy the prickly hedgehog, so I got my summons and I thought, "I'm not accepting three points and a £75 fine".

I was innocent, so I went to court to defend myself and walked away with five points and a £250 fine. Fuckin lying tossers. I was livid.

When I was younger, I was forever paying a fine for one thing or another. It seems that the plod targets the young males to make themselves feel that extra bit macho!

A couple of years ago, I got a phone call from Manchester Police. Apparently, my dozy son had been in the library and left his passport (nothing new for him. I've lost count of the number of mobiles he's lost). The police phoned me because I was next of kin at the back of the passport. I said I would get on to my son and tell him to collect it.

What the copper didn't tell me (because if he had done, I would have gone straight there myself and retrieved it), was that if it wasn't collected the same day, it would be destroyed. What a cunt!

When my son went to retrieve it he was informed that the passport was no longer. I phoned the plod back only to be met with "and?". Fucking "and"! "What a selfish prick you are," I said, "£100 for a new passport, and… and you're a twat!"

Oh my God, I'm right on one now, so here goes. Never let it be said that I don't carry a grudge, because I really do. I've upset a few as well, and I know they say people in glass houses shouldn't throw stones…

One of the best bits of advice I could give to anyone is that it's better to make 50p for doing nothing than a pound for doing everything. And if you never spend more a week than you earn, you'll always have money.

Here are a few bits to leave you with.

The main grudges I carry are when a decision of another affects the lives of others. It doesn't have to affect me, but it still gets my back up.

My first grievance was the decision by Glenn Hoddle to omit the fantastic Paul Gascoigne from the World Cup squad in favour of the young Theo Walcott, who wasn't ever going to make the pitch in a million years. Gazza would have been a great asset to the squad's dressing room, and because of his age, experience and the fact his career was close to the end, would have been great for a 15-minute substitution if England were trailing and in need of a little inspiration. But Hoddle thought he would play GOD in his decision of omission. And, yes, for that decision (and that decision alone) I have a total dislike of him. Such arrogance!

Then we had the so-called tough guy, Stuart Pearce. So what if he was a good player for Nottingham Forest and England. To me, that all went down the pan when he was put in charge of the Great Britain football team for the Olympics, and thought he too would play God. He did this by leaving out of the squad the one man who had campaigned tirelessly for the whole Olympic team, the fantastic ambassador, David Beckham. All because Pearce felt like being the big 'I am'. As it happened, just like Hoddle's England team, they arrived home before the postcards, and that (for the reasons stated earlier) put a large smile on my face. Pair of arseholes.

Seems I must know as much, if not more, about football than them two put together. Ha ha, I love it.

I'm pleased to say that my third and final rant and rave ended with a better story. I was watching Swansea play in the League Cup final of 2013, not something we get to see very often. Swansea did the business and went on to beat Bradford and win the cup five nil. Nathan Dyer had scored two goals already as Swansea were awarded a penalty. No player had ever scored a hat trick in a final in this cup's history. The stage was set for little old Nathan to become the first. Then up pops the most selfish arsehole I've ever seen. Jonathan de Guzman grabbed the ball and wouldn't let it go for love nor money. He robbed Nathan Dyer of his hat trick opportunity. What a wanker. I still hate him to this day, but I'm so happy for Nathan. He ended up on loan at Leicester City for the unbelievable 2015/16 season when Leicester became champions and Nathan won a medal. I'd so love to shove that medal up de Guzman's arse.

One last one to finish. It's a bit closer to home, this one. My daughter was attempting to get into university to study a nursing course. She didn't get in, not because of lack of qualifications but because of a power-tripping tosser who decided they weren't giving her a place. I know what you're saying. "If at first you don't succeed", and, yes that's my motto too, but the arsehole knocked the stuffing from her and robbed her of the opportunity of a better life.

Sorry if I went off track then, and it is nothing to do with comedy, but it's just my opportunity to say my bit. But, fuck it, while I'm on a roll... There was a wanker at the Barclays on Salford Quays and a fuckin bitch at the Nationwide Building Society in Walkden. The Barclays man called my overdraft in at the worst possible time with not one ounce of compassion, the fully fledged knob-headed prick. Then we get to the bitch from the Nationwide (who may I add was only at the branch for a mere two or three months), but saw it in her power to cancel my three accounts I'd held for 30 years. All because she thought she heard me swear at a clerk. Total injustice, and I won't forget, bitch!

That's my rants and advising over!

14
TV WORK

OVER THE YEARS, I'VE MADE SEVERAL TELEVISION appearances, although I never had the chance to appear either telling jokes or playing the drums. I did get to sing, though, albeit on the BBC's *Watchdog* programme.

In the early years, I did lots of extra work.

The included appearances in *Brookside*, *Crossroads* and dramas like *The Gathering Seed* and *Juliet Bravo*, to name but just a few.

When artistes work as extras, they all long for that big break and the chance to get a speaking part. To put it bluntly, most extras would stab their granny for a speaking part, and it's all wrong. Extras really do get treated like shite. I don't think I ever met a director or producer who didn't think the extras at their disposal were second-class citizens. Whether that's true or not, I did (for all my sins) get two breaks. The first was an advert for Jewson's the builders.

I travelled down to London only to end up on the cutting room floor. Even *I* knew how to film it right. But who was I to argue with a director or producer? It kind of stinks when you tell your family and friends to watch out for you only for them to be still watching and waiting some 30 years later. Yes, its deflating and leaves you devastated.

Then I got a three-episode part in *Emmerdale Farm* in 1983. It was nine days work in Leeds, and I played a motorbike lad called Tone. Again, I was unlucky, and my inexperience found me once again on the cutting room floor. Although I was still featured, some of my lines yet again ended up in the director's bin. That was the closest I got to an actual break. I thought it was the beginning of something great. I think I actually believed my agent,

Sylvia Hughes, when she flannelled me with the bullshit, "You could be the next James Bond".

Later, in 1997, I got a spot in a cutting-edge documentary called *The Complainers*. This was a good gig and led to several other spots on various programmes. They, in turn, led to a break as a TV presenter doing a regular spot on a Friday evening for *Granada Tonight*, the north west leading news programme. My part was to run for eight weeks and was going great guns.

A further stint in another cutting-edge documentary *The Rogue Males*, came back to haunt me. It put me not only right back where I started, but even further behind. My big break was taken away from me as quickly as it arrived. A few other TV bits and pieces came and went, but like all things showbizzy, I realised TV wasn't going to happen for me.

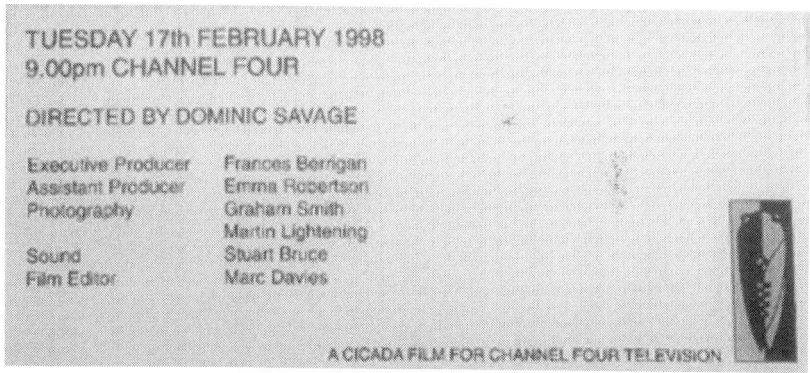

CUTTING EDGE

ROGUE MALES

TUESDAY 17th FEBRUARY 1998
9.00pm CHANNEL FOUR

DIRECTED BY DOMINIC SAVAGE

Executive Producer	Frances Berrigan
Assistant Producer	Emma Robertson
Photography	Graham Smith
	Martin Lightening
Sound	Stuart Bruce
Film Editor	Marc Davies

A CICADA FILM FOR CHANNEL FOUR TELEVISION

I was actually in rehearsal for a Bay City Rollers tribute act when the phone rang and an agent said that a Bay City Rollers tribute was needed for the BBC primetime show *Watchdog*. It was being filmed at St Andrews in Scotland. He asked the question, "Is your band ready?" "Too right," I said. We weren't, but I wasn't passing up the chance, no way. We rehearsed for five hours on the way up to Scotland, all squashed up in the car, and we pulled it off. Good old Ann Robinson introduced us and we performed great. Only we knew that rehearsals only finished three hours earlier. The most amazing fact was that bands spend years rehearsing and gigging to get a television moment. We got one and hadn't even done a gig.

Unreal.

Like everything else, the programme still amounted to nothing, but what the hell, nothing ventured nothing gained. We did it and, as it happened, we were a replacement for the original Bay City Rollers who refused (for whatever reason) to appear. That's a little claim to fame there.

B.C.R, the Bay City Rollers tribute band.
"Bye Bye Baby." Remember "Shang a Lang".

My Premier drum kit in 2016 would have cost a fortune, but knowledge is power.

15
THE ROADIES

OVER THE YEARS I HAD MANY A ROADIE. A ROADIE IS a person who is meant to help in all aspects – do a little driving, help carry in the equipment, watch my back and have their pick of all the free ladies on hand, ha ha, should they want them. Some of the roadies that came with me over the years were either in for the long haul or soon disappeared into the sunset (after realising when they first came that it didn't have the same magic three or four further trips down the line). But, like many a roadie, they all have a story to tell, and their own version of what life was like on the road!

I'm probably not going to remember all the roadies and, should I miss one or two out, I apologise wholeheartedly. I've said on many occasions that I did well to remember as much as I did, ha ha.

I had Lawrence Harrison, a guy I've known since being a kid myself. As kids, he was one of life's original hard boys, though I feel life caught up with him and he'd mellowed out a little. If I'm honest, I think his hard-case image came from his Borstal days.

Another Kersal kid was also a bit of a Cain Dingle-type tough guy by the name of Mike Probert. It's not that these guys were ever needed for the tough guy role. After all, I was just a comic, they weren't watching the back of the president.

Another guy who probably stayed the longest, was Duane Talbot. I reckon I owed him a lot, even though the crafty fucker had a shady side. He stayed alongside me a long time and was responsible for a lot of the memories I bring with me, to this day. I was forever carrying with me a video camera, and when I couldn't be behind the lens it was down to Duane to pick up the camera. It was either a gig or a footie match, most of which he did for free, although I tried to look after him as best as I could. What's more, he had an eye for the ladies, and what better a place to have that eye than being on the road. He certainly got his fair share and had a good run.

George Howarth, my friend and neighbour and an ex bus driver, came on many an occasion, as did ex old bill, John 'Shagger' Shawcross – another red-blooded male who supplied me with a few stories I'll tell you a little further down the line.

Then there was Liam Kenny from Brookhouse in Eccles. Although he came for a while, he was never a driver as he only learnt to drive later on in life when his days as a roadie had passed. The lazy bastard, ha ha, only kidding, Liam. It was down to him I got in at The Cliff, Manchester United's old training ground. That was a time I thoroughly enjoyed, and I met quite a few people. Here's one for Liam. The only time I really needed him to have my back he missed it while having a drink at the bar. Ha ha. He will tell you that he was busy fighting off the other 200 in the vault.

Tony Darcy was another Brookhouse lad. Alongside Rex and Toe's brother Paul (Giro), he came on many an occasion, as well as doing the door on some of the nights where I had promoted the shows. Giro had a little run for a while, moaning bastard that he was.

Around Christmas time each year, I used to promote a Christmas Ladies Night at several venues including Wakefield's Snooker Club in Salford. There, the Eccles lads used to treat it like I needed ten doormen and would bring a minibus full of inebriated lads. Mr Darcy said, "I've brought reinforcements. I got payback on them". It was the funniest thing in the world when I instructed the female crowd to "Go get em, girls".

One guy who came just a couple of times (to be honest, I couldn't afford him any more than that), was Quinny (Mark Quinn). He thought it was hilarious to sell my video tapes and keep the cash, blatantly of course.

David Harrison, another Eccles tanker driver, did a spell and he too had a few stories for me. I also met a guy called Stephen Taylor while working on a house at Bolton doing building work. I later nicknamed him ROCKORD, (he was the spit of Fred Flintstone). He used to come along with me, then later started to tag along with Boy Blue, the male stripper who did most gigs to a female audience. If I was being a roadie, there would be no competition about which gig I would roadie for.

Apparently, though, he met a girl in north Yorkshire, moved in with her, tried to kill her then ended up in jail. I had a few letters from him but we lost touch and I've never heard from him from that day to this. That's well over 20 years ago, but I've still got his letters.

Alan Guest, an agent I used to work for in Yorkshire, was from A&R Entertainments. He was actually an ex-member of The Gutter Band and came often. He will kill me for telling you this, but he too liked a scoop or two, and while carrying two of my big speakers down a flight of stairs and a little worse for wear, he went tumbling down. Oh, we laughed to see such fun and the dish ran away with the spoon. He was a big lad so didn't hurt himself, and my speakers lived to sound another day.

Since I packed it all in and reduced myself to doing the odd gig every blue moon, one guy who never got the chance to get bored by tagging along every now and again, was Conka (aka Mark Smith). He was a bit of a tough cookie, and an ex-football hooligan who was also known on the soccer pitch as 'Thunderbolt Conk', but, fuck me, can that guy moan! And, and as for patience, just forget it. He didn't have the patience to wait for his next breath. He did have a great sense of humour, but liked his scoops, which meant the journey home always took longer because he needed me to stop every five minutes while he emptied his bladder. As I've said before, various people came along a handful of times, including Martin Madden and little Steve Daly (RIP, mate).

My Uncle Jimmy even came once. I picked him up from his cottage in Meliden, near Prestatyn, and he came with me to Anglesey. Boy, was he in his element being surrounded by female strippers.

A big disappointment to me was that my dad, James Frank Parkin, never lived long enough to travel with me, although he would have told me off for the swearing and telling blue gags with my cocky humour.

He would have loved being around the strippers (ha ha), but he wouldn't have approved of my act. As he often said to me, "Sarcasm is the lowest form of wit". Someone finished the sentence off years later: "and, if wit was shit, you'd be constipated". Ha ha.

As far as roadies go, I've named but a handful. I collected a few stories that were from a roadie's point of view, and here are a couple in just a few sentences.

JOHN SHAWCROSS (SHAGGER)

"I went quite a few times with Scully as his sidekick/minder/helper, and have my own few stories to tell. Here's the one memory that has never left me. It was Blackpool Pleasure Beach. Scully had just performed at The Attic and had gone down well. Well enough to attract a few punters who wished to buy a few of his mementos, tapes and t-shirts etc. One guy bought a t-shirt then kept passing and shouting to Scully, 'Top banana, top banana'.

As we were sat at the bar having a quick bevvy, the same guy came back over and asked Scully to sign the back of his purchased t-shirt with 'Top banana'. I couldn't control my laughter when Scully proceeded to sign it with 'I am a twat, now fuck off'. I was howling with laughter."

DAVID HARRISON

In a sentence from David Harrison, the tanker driver from Eccles, he was good enough not to give anything away, clever lad. He said

"I'd love to tell you all the story from Wakefield's Snooker Club in Salford. One Christmas party night…" But, in his words, he stuck with, "We had GREAT NIGHTS OUT, there was never any trouble and we always had a good laugh watching the show. Ba bum."

Thanks David.

They do say everybody's got a story to tell. After a long showbiz career, I certainly have many. Remembering them all is the hard bit, but having spent the day in the company of Vinegar Vera from Salford, it's clear that lady could have filled a book on her own. God bless her. Vinegar Vera RIP.

Then we have the many faces that weren't really roadies. They were people who just tagged along for a night out. That night out provided a change of scenery and a glimpse into the life a lot thought was glamorous. But they discovered it's all roads, motorways and smoky concert rooms, bingo, pies and pasties. Ha ha.

Such people as Neil Chapman, Ian Anderson and his sidekick Alan Macintosh, Dave Faunt, and Steve Daly… The road was also shared with various ladies who relished a night out in a different town or city.

On a slightly different note, another of my favourite ever films was *The Bargee,* starring Ronnie Barker and Harry H Corbett of *Steptoe and Son* fame. It was set a on barge that travelled up and down the canals, and the star, Harry, had virtually a lady in every town. A man after my own heart. Not that I did, of course, but that's a reputation that taints a lot of showbiz people who travel the length and breadth of the country because of their job!

LIAM KENNY

I had continually asked Liam Kenny for a couple of sentences, and was beginning to think he couldn't read or write, because if I'd asked him once I'd asked him a dozen times and I was waiting for ages. The truth is, the fucker couldn't even speak until he was seven years old. Ah well, Liam. You snooze you lose. Liam's been a goalkeeper for most of his footballing life, and I did pen him a song, which turn was dedicated to him. It was called *The Goalkeeper's Kick*, and on top of all that, he shared the stage with both me and our very own Vinegar Vera.

After hearing my book was due for release in October 2022, Liam finally decided to put pen to paper, so here's what he said about being a roadie. By the way, I asked him for ages to write something, and he didn't. Then, when he did, the fucker didn't stop! I informed him afterwards that each page costs £50 to produce, so I had to cut his £480 essay/book to £50! Anyway, thanks Liam!

"So, back in 1995, a large group of friends from the Eccles area went to a Gents Evening at a local venue. The show was meant to consist of a comedian and female exotic dancers, the posh word for strippers. The comedian booked was a skinny guy with a short back and sides haircut, a scrawny, silly-looking moustache, and was dressed from head to toe in a black and white stripy outfit resembling the character, Beetlejuice. The show kicked off and a great laugh was had all round. We laughed more at the fact that one of our mates who was invited to perform with the girls didn't or couldn't. Not that that was a problem to him in real life, but with ten of 15 or your mates egging you on, he probably wouldn't have been alone in that fact, but it was hilarious to see.

I met the comedian again about a year later, at five-a-side football, and, over time, got to know him quite well. I had a longing to be asked to go to one of the shows I'd seen him perform a year earlier. Then I got an invite. It was over to Wrexham for the opposite to a Gents Night. It was a Ladies Night. Again there was a comic, and, in opposite contrast to the female strippers, it was males walking in with the comedian. Had the women thinking I was the male stripper. I smiled and made my apologies. "Sorry, girls, this guy isn't showing anyone his one-inch-wonder."

My role in this evening was not as a paying punter getting intoxicated with alcohol, but to roadie and take care of the comedian and male dancers' requirements, so the stage was all set up. Sound check done. Porn mags and baby oil for the strippers were all in place. My role when the strippers were performing was to protect them from wild females baying for their bodies. But, if I'm honest, only a mental case would come between a horny group of inebriated females and a stripper's todger, so, as much as I was 'head of security' I stood smiling, knowing full well the guys covered in oil were more than capable of handling the sex-craved women.

After going on quite a few of these nights, I got to witness good nights, and the actions that took place. Quite often on a Ladies Night, as an addition to the fun, a raffle would be run, and the winning ticketed women would get to choose from all the men on view, which one they would like as a prize. That man was now theirs to do as much or as little as she chose. Often, when it was my turn to be picked, if she wasn't a looker, I would step aside and let the next man grab her till I got a winning ticket. I'm not saying I'm a George Clooney myself, but on these nights, the women on offer would range from Miss Piggy to Miss World, and I've never yet had my share of pork. Ha ha.

The thing I learnt on a Ladies Night was that it didn't matter if the girls were single, married or in-between. On a night of this calibre, they were up for all kinds of fun and the gents were only too happy to oblige. On most of the shows you could tell virtually straight away if the night was destined to be a good one.

While I enjoyed the Ladies Nights immensely, I didn't enjoy the Gents Nights as much. Stag parties were just a bunch of drunken men, hell bent on outwitting the comedian and physically abusing the female strippers. But, just like the male strippers who handled the females with ease, the female strippers were hard-skinned enough to deal with most men, and in retaliation for their abuse, they would inevitably have the last laugh as they covered them in talc and oil. All the while, their mates would be in hysterics. Watching the girls ruin a guy you can only describe as a prick, was priceless.

I was a roadie/security man for almost seven years, and travelled all over the country. It was very different from a normal daytime job that had you fixed in the same place, day-in- day-out. I got to see places and meet people that almost definitely would never have.

A couple of highlights were The Circus Tavern in Purfleet, Essex. It was a very large cabaret-style venue, and in complete contrast to that was The Unicorn's basement, in my home town of Eccles. I even got to fly to Germany, where the show was entertaining the British Armed Forces. Their faces when we showed up looking like long-haired hippies, and stinking from head to toe, was a picture in itself.

It was a great night, and they invited us for a night out at the barracks, which we had to politely decline as we had a plane to catch back to Manchester. My list of stories could fill a book by themselves, but like most things in life, what happens on the road, stays on the road. Scully gave me the opportunity to travel to places I had only imagined existed, and meeting people I definitely wouldn't have, but there was a best bit.

The best bit was there were some good-looking girls in Eccles, but I got to see good-looking girls in various parts of the country too. My little bonus. In 1982, my daytime job, I started work at Pilkington Tiles, where I met a lot of people and made some good friends. One friend in particular, was a female with whom I confided a little too much information about my life on the road. It turned out to backfire on me, as we later become partners. As a knock on the door came, I came downstairs smelling of Gucci, only to be asked by my Mrs where I was going. 'With Scully,' I said. 'Not on your nelly,' she said. 'I know all about what goes at them nights'. And, that was it. My time on the road was over. Do I miss it? No. Would I do it again? No. Would I change anything? Still no. We had a blast, and those memories too are priceless.

I can't believe that Scully cut my 48 pages to five. Ah, well, I knew that once I started, I wouldn't be able to stop. In truth, what makes me laugh and smile, would only make others rage with jealousy. Ha ha."

Thank you, Liam. We don't see much of each other these days. Liam has a job on the railways which he's had for a few years. Not as glamorous as being a roadie, but nonetheless, it still takes him all over the country. And, like everybody else, we have families that take up our precious time.

I would like to finish with a thank you. I know Liam was grateful for the experience to travel a bit of the country and meet different people to the norm. I appreciated his help, but I was also grateful to him. He played football regularly at The Cliff, the Manchester United training ground, and he gave me the opportunity to go down there and play a bit. I love it. Got to play with better footballers, and meet lots of people. It wouldn't have been possible without his help. That period in my life lasted almost as long as his stint as a roadie with me, and I am eternally grateful. Thank you.

Me, Vinegar Vera and Liam Kenny.

DUANE TALBOT

The roadie that stayed with me the longest was Duane, or as I and a lot of others would say "dddddDuane". He had a slight speech impediment caused by something that happened to him when he was younger. He was a good lad really but a little light-fingered on a few occasions. I put that down to the fact something upstairs was a little bit missing. No offence, my mate, but all in all we've got our faults, be it one thing or another. He wasn't a bad lad, and I will always remain eternally grateful for all the hours he roadied and spent behind the lens of my video camera filming a footie match or a gig. He let me down a fair few times but, on the whole, I can't complain because he did a great job. Because of his speech impediment, he used to pronounce things with a DD. If he was making a brew, he would ask "How many dugars (sugars)?" I'd say "Dugars?" and he would then say "Fuck off", (or maybe it was "Duck off") ha ha. I based a joke on him. It's called *That Won't Keep Till After the Wedding.* It was very apt, though not true, ha ha. Cheers, Duane.

THAT WON'T KEEP TILL AFTER THE WEDDING!

I've got a best mate. Bless him. He's 31, and still a virgin. The poor fucker's never had his leg over.

I know you lot will be thinking, "Fuck me, ya lying". Well, I know they do say there's someone for everyone, and they'd be right. It's just a matter of finding the right match. This is the difficult bit because, believe me, he's no oil painting.

And what's more, he ffuckinn ttalkss llikee tthatt!

So, I so I thought for his birthday I will take him where everybody gets a fuck! Yes, you guessed it. Benidorm! If you can't get your end away there, there's something wrong. You've got the booze, the sun and the chickadees. Oh, my word, it's swarming with wall-to-wall crumpet.

So, I rang Ryanair and sorted the job. We packs our case, hand luggage only of course… Fuck me ya take an extra kilo and they become nasty wasps attempting to sting ya duty free. That's a load o bollocks. Dear as fuck, that shit.

So, we land us bags, go straight into the hotel and were lay there on the beach on our dildos. I mean lilos.

Picture it. The sun beaming down. I'm thinking factor fuck all. Golden suntan. All of a sudden, this chick walks past. Fuck me. Drop dead gorgeous. I'd have sucked a fart straight out of her arse. Beautiful legs, mega tits, gorgeous face. Just as she's passing me, I shout "Hola el e quandos se merie, I'm here".

She smiled. Aww, her teeth were like impeccable. A grand piano. She said "Hi there". I thought, "Oh, my fuckin God, a gorgeous to-die-for chick, and she fuckin talks like him".

Well, as she spoke his eyes popped up so he speaks to her. Well, even though he was no looker, she was impressed with his voice. Fuck me it was "Blah de blah de blah blah de blah de blah". They got on like a house on fire.

Turns out she was a 29-year-old virgin as well. That was it. I didn't get a look in! For them two it was love at first sight. They decided to get married, but made a pact (obviously instigated by her, the bitch) that there would be no sex before the wedding.

So, they're in their hotel bedroom a little worse for wear after jug after jug of the Benidorm brew, Sangria. Slowly, she took off her top. Oh, my word, the most delicious lumps I've ever seen. Well, I was hidden in the wardrobe. I was only curious to see what two virgins were going to get up to.

Scrabble, and shit, my arse, ha ha.

He said "Fuckin ell, what's those?"

She said, "These are my tits".

He said, "Fukinelllll, they're like peaches. Can I have a feel?"

She said, "Oh no, you'll have to wait till after the wedding".

He said "Fukinelll".

Just then he pulled his trunks down. A big 12" unused (apart from wanking) cock fell out. Her eyes bulged out of her tiny gorgeous face.

"Fukinell, what's that big enormous thing?" she said.

"It's me dick,"

She said, "It's a fuckin big bastard that! It's like a golf club! Fukinellll, can I have a stroke?"

He said, "No. a-a-a. You'll have to wait till after the wedding".

She said, "Fukinelllll".

I was pissing me fuckin sides crouched hiding in that fuckin wardrobe.

Just then she pulled down her knickers. The biggest and hairiest beaver known to man was staring back at him.

"Fukinellll, what's that?"

She said, "It's my minge".

He said, "Fukinelllll, it's a hairy bastard innit?"

He stood there looking at it, all proud.

He said, "Can I have a stroke?"

She said, "No".

He said "Fukinellllll. Can I smell it then?"

She said, "Oh, go on then".

He went sniff, sniff, sniff, sniff, before yelling out at the top of his voice.

"FFFFUUUCCKKIIINNNNEEEELLLLLL. That won't keep till after the wedding…"

Duane Talbot.

16
SPORTSMENS DINNERS

OF ALL THE GIGS I EVER DID, MY LEAST FAVOURITE of all were the Sportsmans Dinners. In case you're unsure, a Sportsman's Dinner usually consisted of a room full of men, with the odd woman. The men would be shirt-and-tied-up, having a three-course meal and dipping in their pockets for raffles, auctions and whatever other fundraising activities happened to be going on at the time. All events were different and held for a different purpose. The room was usually set with a top table, and on the top table would be the entertainment for the night. Usually, it would consist of a compere/anchorman, a comedian, and a guest speaker or speakers.

It was the usual to expect and have the entertainment all sitting together on that top table. One by one, each would stand and do his turn. I found this format very uncomfortable. I hated being sat at a table with everyone, then having to stand and ridicule those I'd just been socialising with. It was difficult. For most comedians, it wouldn't be a problem, but I was a blue, mickey-taking comic who left no one off the radar. Everybody was fair game.

Over the years I did many of these gigs, but not nearly as many as other comics. I tried my best to steer clear. In the early days, I worked with some sporting greats, Nobby Stiles, John Conteh, and Duncan Mackenzie, who I helped rescue from a crowd of heckling idiots. He didn't have the ammunition to deal with them, so I obliged – to the delight of the rest of the crowd.

> **SPORTSMANS DINNER**
> at
> **Ashton United Social Club**
>
> Wednesday 21st October 1998
>
> Presented by: Ray Lee
> Master of Ceremonies: John Milne
> Guest Speaker: Duncan McKenzie
> and
> Scully (comedian)

My most uncomfortable night was with the England and Leeds United legend, Mr Jack Charlton. He did his speech and it went down well, but then he thought it was still OK to keep opening his big fat gob during my performance. I had the microphone, yet you could still hear him above me. So, I slated him and, yes, you guessed it, the crowd turned on me. How dare I verbally abuse their hero? (Please see page 226.)

In the later years, I worked with Paul Merson who told me he had some of his books in the boot of his car. They were his autobiography. "They're no good there," I said, "Bring them in and I will get them flogged". I asked, "How many you got with you?" "Ten," he said. "You mean nine, ha ha," cheers, Paul. Well, if you don't ask, you don't get.

Next up was Matt le Tissier, a nice and funny guy who told some funny stories in his laid-back way.

I had the pleasure of sharing the stage next with Lee Sharpe. His reminiscences of the old days and battles with Fergie were hilarious.

Me, Lee Sharpe and my old mate, Ben, the ex– Manchester United groundsman who was Lee's good mate.

It was at my old mate, Shagger's pub in Helmshore, Rossendale. Lee's routine was second to none, as he came out with some belters.

On another show at the same place, we had the pleasure of not one, but four Manchester United legends. For me, that was surreal.

Alex Stepney, John Aston, Pat Crerand and Arthur Albiston… being a lifelong, Manchester United fan, you can imagine I was in my element, being surrounded by the team's legends.

The safe hands of Alex Stepney.

I was never ever far away from either Old Trafford or The Cliff, Manchester United's Salford-based training ground, where (I'm pleased to brag and name drop), I used to play many a game with the likes of Jimmy Ryan. Yes, Jimmy Ryan from the 1968 European Cup winning squad. That guy may have been 60-odd at the time, but boy could he still play. His first touch and eye for goal was just unbelievable. I graced the pitch with the moaning bastard, Martin Buchan (loved him though), and Scott McGarvey, another nice guy. My most treasured moment that's still stuck in my head was the day Fergie came off and I went on for him, just after he had netted the winner. Yeah!

I even got my own Typhoo Tea card!

Scully's Job Lot at The Cliff.

There's a lot of names I worked alongside. It's not easy to remember. After all, I can't remember last week's football results so there's no surprise there. Tommy Smith, the Liverpool hard man said he will kick fuck out of me if he doesn't get a mention, so this is me mentioning Tommy Smith as well ha ha.

Talking about the sportsmen who do the dinners, not all are the same. Some turn up with a great act in their locker, where others (who are not so used to the speaking scene), turn up to collect their usually large fees, by doing a Q and A. That's answering questions from the audience. It's not fair really, but who am I to say what's right and wrong?

My final dinners saw work with Jamie Moore, Adrian Morley, Steve Howey, and a few final dinners with even more of Manchester United's growing army of legends. There was little Lou Macari, who came fully loaded with his trusted sidekick, Nello (Neil Baldwin). Then it was Sammy McElroy, David May, and the Welshman, Mr Clayton Blackmore.

Me and little old Lou Macari .

I also had the pleasure of working with Norman Hunter and the Chelsea legend Ron 'Chopper' Harris. It was like a re-run of that famous 1970 FA Cup final, a fantastic game that I remember as if it were yesterday.

I was an avid Manchester United fan, but I still remember most of the players from both teams. Norman Hunter was fine and a nice guy but, if I'm honest, me and Ron didn't see eye to eye. I still wouldn't argue with him. He still looks the same old 'Chopper' Harris.

Above: With the legend, Paddy Crerand.
Below: With John Aston.

This is how I remember Pat and John.

PAT CRERAND

JOHN ASTON

Arthur Albiston politely stood in for the not so well David Sadler.

I recently worked with Steve Howey, the ex-Manchester City and Newcastle player. It was a dinner at Bury Cricket Club. I was a bit sceptical of the job and almost cancelled a couple of days before, because I hadn't done a full stand-up spot for a long time. The gags just weren't in my head. The crowd were mostly older guys and I thought they may just not take to my style of comedy and humour. I needn't have worried.

I stormed the place. Once I got going, I was in full swing and they were a great crowd who responded to everything I said. It made my job a little easier. I finished with 'The roadie who talked like that', and the 'Two dogs shagging' gags. Great gags.

Cheers to Eric from Gulliver's for putting me forward for that little gem. Steve Howey did well too, but the cook! I'd sack her on the spot. Ha ha.

Scully and Mr Howey.

All in all, I've had some great Manchester United memories, I've played football at The Cliff, and have been many a time to

Old Trafford. There was even a 'Scully For Manager' banner at the game against Chelsea in the 1980s. I met umpteen of their players, played soccer with a whole bunch (some against and some on the same team), worked alongside a whole host on the dinner circuit, and even shared a laugh or two with a couple.

I almost forgot a few things. I did a gents' do in Prestwich with Tommy Booth, the Manchester City player. I gave him a free DVD of my act and, like a true gent on the football field, he threw it straight back to me.

"Stick it up your arse," he said.

No offence meant nor taken.

Over in Blackburn, I did a Sunday lunchtime show where Joe Corrigan was amongst the crowd. Joe was the butt of my jokes that day and, like the true gent he is, he came back stage to shake my hand. Nice one, Joe.

They do say never judge a book by its cover. Somebody just meeting me today for the first time would be clueless to my past, but I've had a colourful one. I've certainly been there, done that, and worn the t-shirt.

Talking of sport, I may have been a jack of all trades, but I was never a master of one. I could play any sport and did. Football, golf, cross country, tennis, squash, rugby, cricket, badminton, athletics and swimming… I even did a little boxing, but couldn't fight for toffee. I used to get beat up by girls. Deborah Bird, for one, though it was worth a crack just to feel those whopping melons as we rolled around the floor. Ha ha!

I played football for Blackfriars Road Juniors, Lower Kersal, Salford Grammar, Buile Hill High, The Jolly Carter, The Star, The Packet, then The Grapes at Prestwich, the Manchester United Staff Team at The Cliff, and finally, Scully's Job Lot, which was my own team. I was the boss.

MISSED THE BOAT

LEFT: Me as a youngster.

BELOW: Still loving and playing football at the big '40'.

And so, to the school's 1500 metres (see picture above).

I'm on the left, Chris Golley is to my right, and behind us both are Bill Calderbank then Mark Garrod. Not sure who Mr Fifth Place is. Fudd Harwood is next and at the back is Simon Gore.

I did five-a-side at Eccles Rec and the JJB and 11-a-side for Prestwich Heys on the Monday night astra pitch, virtually retiring from football in 2015.

MISSED THE BOAT

My last Sportsmans Dinners in 2017 and 2018.
ABOVE: With David May. BELOW: With Clayton Blackmore.

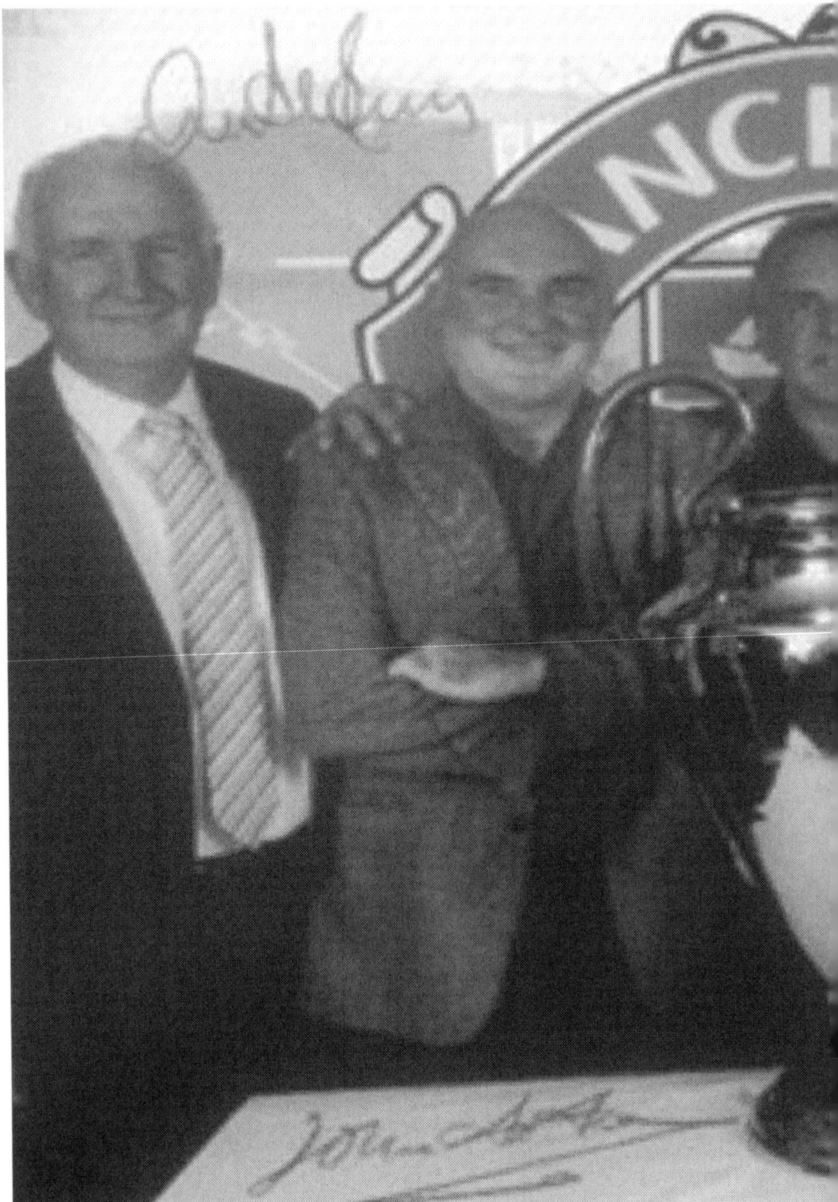

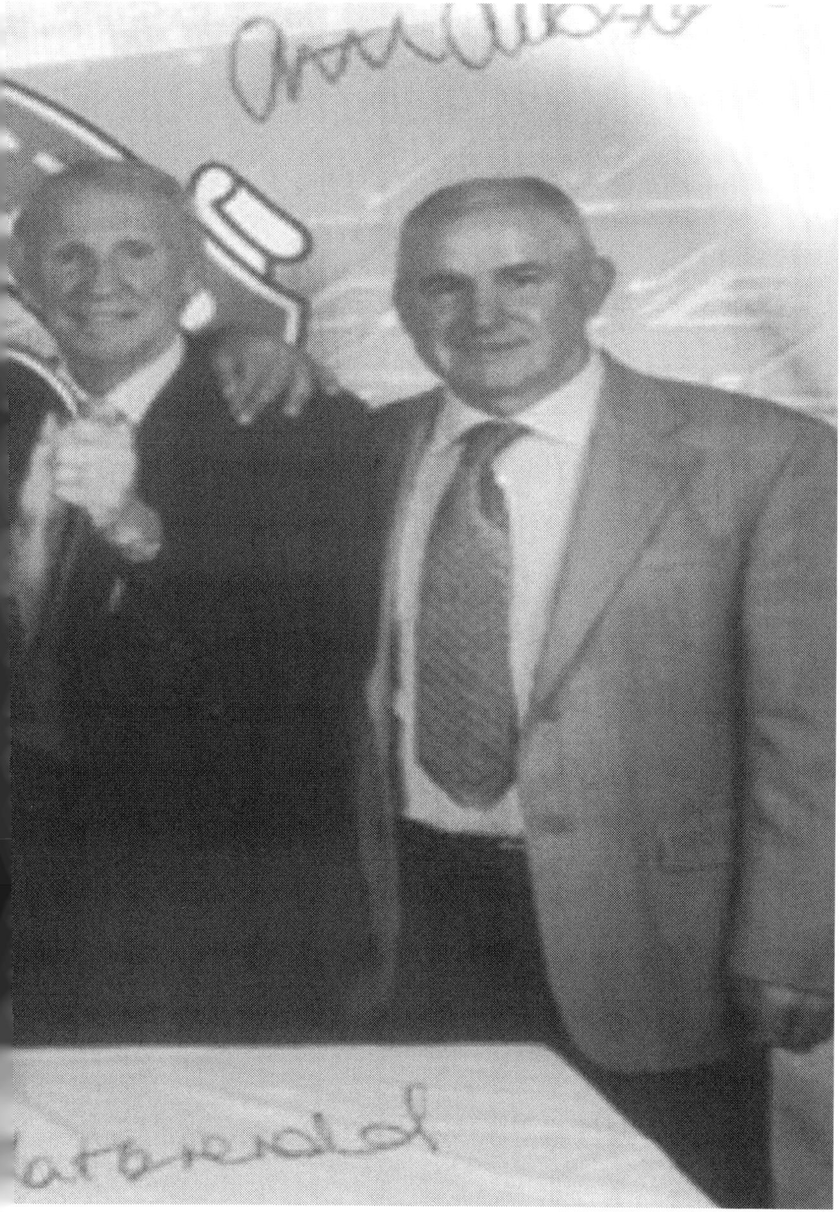

And, Oh, Sammy, Sammy, Sammy, Sammy, Sammy, Sammy McIlroy.

I mentioned on page 207 how I had a dislike for Sir Jack Charlton and how I thought he was rude. However, having watched a documentary film in 2020 titled Finding Jack Charlton, I realised how wrong I was to judge him rude. He was just being Jack. Had I known him personally I would have totally realised it and not made the issue so personal. Apologies, Big Jack. RIP.

17
MATERIAL

WHEN YOU FIRST START OUT WORKING as a comic, you couldn't possibly set off with all your own original material and expect to see out your performance.

I'm pretty sure you'd be booed off the stage, so you start your comedic career with a whole bunch of gags you've put together from whoever or whatever. You have watched and heard it performed, then as the months and years, along with the performances go by, you begin to put your own routines, sketches and jokes together. And that determines your own style and originality.

I'm certainly not embarrassed to say this, but when I started out, I wasn't capable of putting my own stuff together. I didn't have the lifetime of knowledge, nor the talent and skill, so I watched and recorded all the acts I could. This enabled me to build up a routine that I could perform.

As I was working with a band, singing, (my progression from being a drummer), I would start telling the gags between the songs. As I built up my routines, the gaps between songs got longer and longer. In some cases, the other band members would down tools and go off the stage to have a beer while I stayed on doing gag after gag after gag.

All the artistes I had been out there watching had taken years to perfect their acts, jokes and routines. By taking their ideas for myself, I realised I could do it in weeks. That was my way of learning from them.

My act consisted of routines that were intertwined with one-liners, mickey-takes and heckler gags. I also used to parody songs as well, taking a well-known song and switching the words.

I wasn't satisfied with just being a comic and writing comedy material. I also loved to sing.

I wasn't kidding myself or anybody else that I had a voice. I didn't for one minute think I had, but that didn't stop me belting out a tune or even writing songs.

As a comic, I opened my show with a parody – a famous song where I changed the lyrics. I had many a favourite over the years.

I'm a Believer was my first, then it was *Tell Her About It*, the Billy Joel song. Next came the KC and the Sunshine Band track, *Baby, Give It Up*, on to an Elvis number with *That's Alright Now, Mamma*, and *Let Me Entertain You* by Robbie Williams. The funniest by a long way was my parody of *Mambo no 5*. I also did two from Cliff Richards' large repertoire, *The Young Ones* and *Wired for Sound*.

One of the downfalls to using another comic's gags was that if he or she had made it their own by it being out there on a recording, you would from time to time come across an audience member who was familiar with that fact. They would not be shy in letting you know.

I swear, in all my years, the one comic I got that for the most was Chubby

Brown, and that was because his first couple of tapes were flooded into the market place. If you told one gag off those tapes in one of every ten gigs, you would hear a punter shout, "Chubby Brown!". There were two particular lines that it seemed everybody knew.

"Your fanny's big, isn't it? Isn't it? Isn't it? Isn't it?

"There's no ne need to repeat everything."

"I didn't love, that was an echo."

And the other...

"The size of your fanny, love, you could have had carpets fitted".

It was kind of frustrating, but you just had to grin and bear it. It may not have been one of his original lines but because he put them out there first, he got the credit. Sod's law, I'm afraid.

Over the years I've written dozens of songs. I'm not saying they aren't good, but then I'm no Paul McCartney or Lionel

Ritchie either. I did make it into the studio countless times over the years, and made both lyrical and instrumental recordings of my songs.

In the early days I did a single, *Why Are We Here?* coincidentally the title of the screenplay I've written that's still being pushed.

The next big thing.

Why Are We Here? - the 45 single, recorded in 1985 cost me over £1000. An up to date version was recorded in 2017, sung by John Prendergast.

MISSED THE BOAT

As I mentioned in this section, the tapes sold by Chubby Brown to bring his jokes to a wider audience were all part of the bigger picture of merchandising. It was a bandwagon I hit onto pretty quickly. I started with tapes, badges, t-shirts (eight different ones), to statues and even bars of rock, little joke books, then DVDs, posters, photos and scarves.

My joke book from 1992. A 32 page pocket-sized book full of jokes and photos.

18
HARRY BARNES

MY OLD MATE, HARRY BARNES, (WHO IS still my mate to this day), gave me my first comic job at the Belle Vue Lake Hotel. It was on a Sunday afternoon with John Robinson junior, a very well established, Manchester-based comedian. He was also very funny, could sing and was very good at impressions.

He was working on a Gentlemens Afternoon with female strippers and he gracefully allowed me to do a 25-minute spot. Obviously, after he had performed of course. I mean, he was good, but not mental.

I later returned that type of favour on a show in Liverpool, not to him but to none other than Miss Crissy Rock, the comedienne and actress. May I add that she went on to greater fame, doing all sorts of television work including Granada TV's *Benidorm* and the lead role in a great film called *Ladybird Ladybird*. I was the comic on a Gents' Night and Crissy was just starting her act as a comedienne.

So up she got, just like I did all those years before. I later worked with Crissy near Southport where she was the comedienne and I was the stripper in the *Full Monty* Troupe. It was a complete role reversal. You couldn't write this stuff. Oh yes, I am, ha ha.

Miss Crissy Rock!

I'll always remember when I was the front man in a band I'd put together called Jade. I was singing and telling jokes alongside Dave on drums, Phil on guitar, John Martin on bass and the two female backing singers, Janet from Stockport and Susie Valli from Hyde.

The more I strung the gags together, working with the band, the bigger the gaps grew between songs. That meant the more frustrated the band members became, and it got to the point where they just wanted to gag me.

We got many of our gigs from various agents but the majority came from Harry Barnes Entertainments. And it was Harry, no less, who said the immortal words, "You'll end up a comedian".

"No, I won't", I said, "I like doing this".

But, when you realise that as a comedian, you can get paid as much as the whole band put together, and on top of that you only have yourself to deal with, well, I'm afraid that too is a no-brainer.

Henceforth, Mr Barnes was right. A comic was born and his name was Scully.

He's a good lad is Harry. He was an agent who put my bread and butter on the table for many, as well as being a fellow comedian.

He was Naughty Norman when he worked on the Ladies Nights, and Marty Jones when he did the Gents Nights. He also worked as a DJ too, but I've no idea of his name, or what he called himself when spinning discs. Ha ha.

Boy, over the years did I give him some shit. How he tolerated me, God only knows, because I never will. I used to be forever on his case about how he should be pushing me and offering me first dibs on all the work that came into his office.

Yes, I was one cheeky mother Fokker. I probably felt an entitlement because he was my mate. I've known Harry a long time both as a work colleague and friend, and on that note, I would like to say a massive thank you for being both.

Harry Barnes, AKA Marty Jones and Naughty Norman.

Wishing him all the luck for the future.

There's one thing about Harry I would just like to mention. When I say he's a bright spark, I don't just mean he's an electrician, although he is a fully qualified spark, but over the years he has invented a couple of things. Like all good inventions, if you don't have the financial muscle or the backup team your idea either gets nicked by someone else or falls to the wayside .

A long time ago, Harry came up with an idea for cameras in the goalposts to determine if a ball had fully crossed the line. He named it *Goalminder*, and it would prove beyond all shadow of a doubt that it was a goal. But, after sinking his entire available fortune plus may I add other peoples into it, it still wasn't enough to convince the football powers that be, that his idea goalminder was the best. Instead, he missed out as they went with a company who already had a foot in the door through various other projects.

I really felt for him on that one, but he's still here and still inventing.

Good on you, mate.

The smiling Harry Barnes.

So, I felt it was only right to let Harry have his say on his journey so far. Harry? Harry…? Harry! For all his inventions, he's not found a pen and paper. Hang on. Hold the headlines. He's made it…

"Harold Barnes was born on the same day as John Travolta – the 18th of February 1954. As well as being an electrician, Harry has tried his hand at being a theatrical agent, a stand-up comedian, a DJ and scooter enthusiast.

In Harry's world of comedy, he was lucky to have graced the same stage as Laurel and Hardy, at the Theatre Royal in Hanley, as well as working both The Talk of the North, and The Frontier at Batley (which incidentally used to be named Batley Variety Club).

Harry has also got the luxury of being able to reminisce over the "I've done that, worked there, and died a death in that place" scenario.

GOALMINDER

Goalminder was goal line technology invented by Harry in 1998. Incidentally, this was two whole years before Hawkeye clinched the market with their interpretation.

As far as being an entertainments agent is concerned, Harry missed out on the chance to manage Lee Evans, and two of his managed acts made the shortlist for Take That. He did, however manage Bob Williamson for six years, and the world-renowned P.J. Proby for a whole fortnight.

Harry's agency may well have made it on stage with the big players, had it not been for Clive Anderson pulling a show at the last minute, thus causing Harry's agency to end up at the back of the queue to start all over again. He neither had the time nor the inclination to start all over again."

Big Thanks, H.

19
JUST DO US HALF AN HOUR

BEING A STAND-UP COMEDIAN HAD ITS ADVANTAGES, one of them being that you didn't need a single tool to ply your trade. It came from what the man upstairs gave you for free – your voice. Though that was its advantage, it's one biggest disadvantage (and a real pet hate of mine) was that people always looked upon you as their chance for a free dollop of entertainment. Many a time I heard those immortal words, "Will you just do us half an hour?" Like it's that simple. No excuse was good enough.

"Sorry, mate, I'm on a night out with the missus."

"Awww, come on, you'll brighten up the place. That DJ we booked is shite!"

Sometimes, that sentence was all I ever heard.

I remember going to a wedding in Denton with a friend called Maureen. We only went to the night time event, and had barely been in room for ten minutes, and just enough to have got ourselves a beer, when Maureen's friend, the bride, came over. She recognised me as a comedian she had seen working. Apparently, she loved every minute of my performance and did her very best to try and convince me the one thing needed to liven up her dull wedding event was a very little spot from me.

"Oh, go on, please. Will you just do us half an hour?" she said, again and again.

If there was ever a function that I didn't relish working (especially for free) it was a wedding. The reason is, in this day and age, you can never please everybody. Also, with my act at a wedding, you rarely please *anybody*.

I refused. "Sorry, love, I can't perform at a wedding. People are here for a good time, the last thing I want to do is cause an atmosphere and spoil the occasion". "Awww, please... They will love it!"

Again, I declined, but that fell on deaf ears.

Ten minutes later, I heard the DJ announce, "Well, ladies and gentlemen… in ten minutes time were going to be entertained with laughter. We have a comedian called Scully in the room!"

I was embarrassed and wanted to curl up in the corner. Then, on top of that, as if to add insult to injury, the groom (on hearing the announcement) headed straight to me and politely whispered into my ear, "If you say one swear word, I'm going to rip your head off".

Nice. I'm a blue comedian whose whole act is based around foul language, and I was under pressure to be funny and clean at the drop of a hat. Needless to say, at the end of the performance I could hear several elements on one side of the room saying, "I thought he was supposed to be funny!"

"Wrong place, wrong time", is all I had in reply.

That wedding was just one of the ones I didn't like, but on other occasions I've volunteered my services for free to sometimes help a dire situation.

I've been at many a function when there's been no organisation and a DJ that couldn't say boo to a goose. In these cases, I've been more than happy to take over his microphone, sometimes just getting the host up to say a few 'Thank you's and do a speech is all it takes and just helps the night all round.

A blue comic is not what a wedding needs. Laughing at a wedding, or was I crying?

20
ONE LAST SHOT

IT'S ON MY MIND WHETHER I GIVE IT ONE LAST SHOT (in the hope I may get that break), or should I bow out of the showbiz world gracefully and accept that I missed the boat?

At the time I was thinking about calling it a day, the following song wasn't out. But on this day, I'm sat here, writing this paragraph, it well and truly is. So, I can say without further ado

"Let it goooooo …let it gooooooo."

When it comes to fame and fortune in the good old world of showbiz, there's one thing that's always lingering on my mind, and it is TIME.

Time is so precious and it is flying by me at a rate of knots.

I always said to myself that I didn't want to still be performing when I was old and grey. I've seen some artistes still performing who just don't know when to call it a day.

There is the smallest of chances that I may well be forced out of retirement for a special gig! A gentleman, who by the skin of his teeth is still hanging in there, supposedly booked me for his wake. Good old Harry Lomas. Bless him, he's booked me to tell a few gags at his funeral, or was that just another one of my genius stunts to attract publicity? Either way, I commanded a full half page in a daily paper yet again!

Over the last few years I've learnt to live on less money per week, which helps. It means I don't have to scour for as much work as I used to. It isn't easy to live that way, but pensioners do it quite easily, as it happens. And, do you know, when all is said and done, the way I see it is... the more you earn, the more you spend. I also put a theory on that too. It's called unnecessary spending, buying stuff you don't need or will end up not using. It's a waste. Guilty, your honour.

And here's another one for you. With all my offspring, who in this day and age all earn a lot more than I do, when they want to borrow a few quid, one guess whose door they come knocking on for a borrow. Yes, mine! The good old wise owl that is their dad. When it comes to finding fame and fortune in the world of showbiz, I guess I should be happy with what I have, what I've done, and most importantly, where I've been.

The funny and ironic thing is that I'm sat here pondering and dismissing those very thoughts of one last shot, yet I'm sat here writing this book, and, may I add, several others too. My 'biggie' is a screenplay, and I have hope and aspirations of convincing one of the big-boy film studios to take a gamble and produce.

I'm fairly certain it could be a hit. I've visualised, eaten, slept and breathed every scene. I can picture the whole movie, and, when I put it alongside films like *Four Weddings and a Funeral*, *Love Actually*, *The Holiday*, and *Eric*, I can see my film as a HIT. Not that the titles mentioned are films that are no good, and that my screenplay is... They are all good films, but I can see mine as being the same, or as good, if not even better. And, and to make things seem they are on an even keel, my screenplay is almost a true story.

So, I suppose I've never really given up.

I'm just going in a different direction.

Maybe now I'll say that I've missed the plane, the train, or just the plain old simple automobile, ha ha.

Before I finish, I want to tell you that it's always been an ambition of mine to play in a pantomime ("Oh, no, it hasn't!"). In 2006, I was within an inch of doing my first. It was an amateur company based in Worsley, doing their own version of *Robinson Crusoe*.

I was in mid-rehearsal when an audition came up for a part in a musical written by Micky Dacks at the Lowry Theatre. I got offered the part of Murphy in *INNITT*, so I gave my pantomime part to my mate, Harry Barnes. *INNITT* was a 2007, ten-day run musical at the Lowry in Salford. It was a great experience and I met some very nice people too. There's a reunion on the cards very soon.

In 2015 I appeared in *A Christmas Carol* at The Plaza in Stockport. I can say I would have almost enjoyed that if it weren't for the way the company putting it on was run. I completely fell out with them all four days prior to our full week of performances. It was over their decision to play Scrooge themselves over complimentary tickets to those performances with attendances at 35 and 40% of their capacity. Talk about biting the hand that feeds.

Yes, we were working for free. In fact, it wasn't free. It cost us. Three months rehearsing.

I worked out the hours I spent rehearsing, the cost of petrol then the hours of performing at £10 an hour, I would have made at least £1500. Instead, I made nothing, not one measly penny, and all I asked was for six complimentary tickets to one performance. There were 6,000 empty seats over all the performances and there was not one free ticket.

In true Scully fashion, I'm going to say it…

"Fuckin Wankers".

On a final note, I'm fully aware that I was only a comedian, singer and drummer, and not a messiah! I had no God-given rights to anything else for my sins. At best, I was an ordinary person, and at worst I was a nobody, but hopefully, with the little bits I did do, there was enough to leave behind for a future society to take a little notice of.

I'm meaning that my time spent on this God-given planet was not a complete waste.

When I started to write this book over two years ago, it was my intention never to grace a stage again. But, in those two years I have, in the August of 2018 just compered a Sportsmans Dinner, with no other than Frankie Allen the comedian, and the speaker and ex-footballer, Duncan Mackenzie, with whom I worked twenty years ago and mentioned earlier in this book. I did my little MCing bit, then went into The Vault to watch Manchester United versus Leicester, the first match of the new season. Then, at 10 o'clock, I went home, missing both the speaker's and comedian's performances.

But I'd seen them umpteen times, so couldn't be mithered that I may miss something.

So, to my final piece. As mentioned earlier, in 1985, I was part of a comedy showband called Spottymolldoon, and in Failsworth, Manchester, we worked on a presentation night with a very talented and well known comedian called Jimmy Carol. As I departed from the band a year or two later to pursue my own career as a comedian, it was the inspiration of Jimmy Carol that not only spurred me on, but showed me the type of style and material I wanted to perform. Needless to say, as my popularity grew very rapidly, our paths never crossed but it was common knowledge that he wasn't impressed with my standings or the use of his material. Although it never hindered my ability to get work, it did close certain doors.

Two years ago, I made contact with Jimmy through Facebook, with an offer to let him have the video of his show we managed to record on that night in 1985. Basically, there were no hard feelings, and certainly not from me as I complimented him on being my inspiration.

So, on a different note, and right back in the August of 2018, I am organising a charity fund raiser for Jimmy Carol whose showbiz career was cut short in a split second of madness. A brilliant and fantastic comedian who not only inspired me, but made many a person laugh..

WEDNESDAY 29th AUGUST
A SPECIAL BENEFIT EVENING FOR
FEATURING SOME OF THE BIGGEST ACTS FROM THE
JIMMY
CAROL
NORTH WESTS TRIBUTE & COMEDY SCENE + MORE
BLUES BROTHERS
ON A MISSION
ELO TRIBUTE
YOUR COMPERES TONY MARTIN & SCULLY
BCB
Chris
Perry

Now at this time of writing, I have still not had it confirmed that alien life from another planet really does exist. I am a firm believer and I stand alongside a lot of others, but for all the sightings, stories, and mysteries, we still don't have concrete evidence, be it in picture form or scribble.

But, with a little hope and a few prayers, I live for the moment, and hope that I will be around for it, and even longer after it is finally confirmed.

Allan David Birkin, AKA Adge, Alber, Birky, Scully, Albert and Spottymolldoon.

Oh, and Rupert (apparently).

And this is me now hanging up my boots!

Tatty Bye then.

Me, this very day, 2018.

ILLUSTRATIONS AND CREDITS

Though all the photos used in this book were re-taken by Allan Birkin for use in this book, some of the original sources are unknown. Please accept my apologies if you are not mentioned or we have used a photo without your permission. Thank you so much.

Front cover Sydney Harbour, by Allan Birkin, 2013.
Back cover features Shani, Ashley, and Allan Birkin junior.
Special thanks to all who made a contribution.

Muchos gracias.
Allan Birkin.
(The Very Amateur Furrytographer)
2018

THE AUTHOR

Allan David Birkin.
Born 18th September, 1960,
Lower Broughton, in Salford, UK.
Lived on Gallemore Street.
Went to Blackfriars Road Junior.
Moved to Lower Kersal.
One year of Lower Kersal Junior School.
Passed the 11-Plus and went to
Salford Grammar School.
Changed to Buile Hill High School
Did Joinery Apprenticeship with Shepherd Construction, based in Cornbrook, Manchester.
Did six months with Salford Council.
Since then, been self-employed as drummer, singer and comic, alongside being a builder during the day.
Many different roles on TV.
As Allan nears the end of his fifties, he is choosing to put pen to paper about his life in showbiz.

Special thanks over the years to Arthur Waite and Jim Cartwright (photographers), Harry Barnes, Henry Harrison, Alan Guest and all the agents who put bread and butter on my dinner table.

Thanks also go to all the acts and musicians I worked with, the male and female strippers I watched haha, the roadies that kept my journies sane, the landlords, landladies and committee members that let me perform at their venues, and last, but by no means least, all my family and friends

xxxxx

ALLAN BIRKIN

At the present moment, the author has no further titles available for purchase, but please email adb180960@hotmail.com with any enquiries regarding this book or future titles.

COMING SOON!

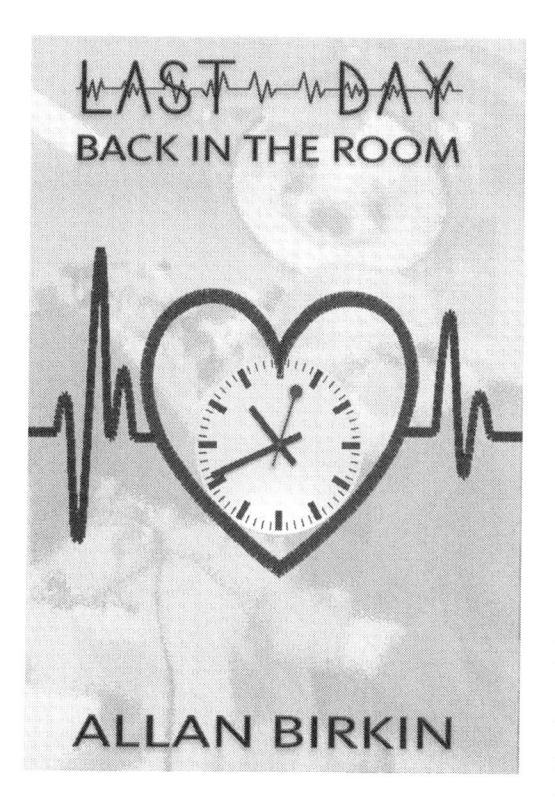

It has always been in my thoughts that the body is like a well-oiled machine and not to be tampered with. Unfortunately, not everyone can go through life without having some form of procedure or another. Although I'd been lucky to never have had to undergo such, when it came to my time for an operation, I couldn't help but have all sorts of thoughts and feelings race through my mind and body. I was being put to sleep. What if I didn't wake up? It has been known. I thought, "What if this is my very last day?" Well, I count myself as very lucky because (after an eight-hour heart operation) I came back into the room. It wasn't my last day, so I'm here to tell the story of my journey that began when I found out my problem, and ends at where I find myself today".

Printed in Great Britain
by Amazon